GW00499598

THE BOOK OF
CHITTLEHAMPTON

THE BOOK OF
CHITTLEHAMPTON

A NORTH DEVON PARISH

HALSGROVE

First published in Great Britain in 2000

Copyright © 2000 Chittlehampton Book Group

DEDICATION

This book is dedicated to all the inhabitants
of the parish – past and present – who have
influenced its culture and development.

British Library Cataloguing-in-Publication Data
A CIP record for this title is available from the British Library

ISBN 1 84114 057 0

HALSGROVE
PUBLISHING, MEDIA AND DISTRIBUTION

Halsgrove House
Lower Moor Way
Tiverton, Devon EX16 6SS
Tel: 01884 243242
Fax: 01884 243325
email: sales@halsgrove.com
website: http://www.halsgrove.com

Initial layout design: xheight Design
Editor: Rae Knight
Picture Editor: John Andow

Printed and bound in Great Britain by Bookcraft Ltd., Midsomer Norton.

Contents

© Mark Slape

Acknowledgements

This book would not have been possible without the help and support of those who live in the parish and, indeed, those who have moved away from here. Our special thanks to those who have lent photographs, letters and other memorabilia, as well as to those who have spent time remembering how things were. Thanks too to those who have given their thoughts on the future of this community and its way of life:

Hazel Alford, Joan Barrow, Colin and Audrey Bawden, Roger Bickley, Gordon and Kathleen Burgess, Bill Castle, Bernard Chambers, Chittlehampton Village Hall, Ross Cockram, Tracey Craze, Judith Domleo, Diane Drummond, Reverend Stephen Girling, Fred Glover, Clifford Gregory, Victor Harris, Carole Henderson-Begg, Marian Howard, David and Helena Johnson, Frank Kidwell, May Lethbridge, Phyllis Lewis, Trevor Martin, The Methodist Rooms, Anthony Murch, Pat Murch, Barry Murch, Dan and Edna Murch, Hazel Needs, Mary Parker, Greta Parkhouse, Phil and Alex Pawley, Kenneth and Nannette Peters, Rosemary Peters, Tony and Dawn Phillips, Ruth Phillips, David and Susan Reed, David Ryall, Bill Seague, Mark Slape, Lorna Southcombe, John Symons, John Thomas, John Webber, Percy Wheaton, Jim White, Lillian Wythe.

Thanks to Richard Lethbridge for lending photographs, supplying old newspaper cuttings and patiently recording interviews. And where would I have been without the dogged good humour and typing skills of Joy Bruce? Major Peter Wood supported me, ghosted for me, and gave me much valued research.

It has not been possible to obtain all the names of those photographed. Readers may wish to fill in those names they recognise in the square brackets [   ] which occur from time to time.

RAE KNIGHT
EDITOR

THE STEERING GROUP:
John Hosking (Chairman);
Diana Murch and Jennie Yule (Secretaries);
Stella Levy (Treasurer and Fund-Raiser);
Roger Cockram;
Stephen Cooke;
John Andow and Marion Edwards.

Foreword

by The Lord Clinton

Risdon in the *Survey of Devon* printed in 1714 describes the Parish of Chittlehampton as being 'graced with a Fair Church and Stately Tower'.

I feel very honoured to write a short foreword to this excellent book. The Rolle and Clinton families have had a long association with the parish and although this is not so much the case as once was, this volume is still of great interest to the family.

It is very important at the start of a new century that a record of events of village life and history are put down in writing and it is through this book that this has been so diligently achieved. I hope that you will find the book as interesting as I have.

Above: *'Drawn in Nature and on Stone' by W. Spreat.*

Introduction

This book is a living collection of the memories, the feelings and the optimism of the people of Chittlehampton and Umberleigh, a parish in North Devon.

A strong sense of community here binds those of very different age, style, occupation and outlook, though there are reminders that this once valuable way of life is giving way to a new one in which communities are changing. Families are dispersed as travel and communication become more accessible, and the lifetime experience once handed on is scarcely heeded now as agriculture struggles to survive and the lure of the internet grows. When sons and daughters leave to work away or marry and maybe emigrate, they take with them photographs and other small family mementoes. In other towns or other countries, those photographs – unmarked – may seem to be of no significance, but here, in the place where they were recorded, they invoke strong memories and serve to remind those who remain of life as it was, and stimulate the talk of how it is now.

Reading these essays or word pictures will convey a real and much larger sense of life in a rural parish today than any clinical analysis might do.

We are so well used now to the bright self-assurance of advertising brochures, to glossy television commercials telling of unparalleled satisfaction, and even to soap operas breathing their analgesic of community life seen through curiously distorted spectacles, that the real thing is in danger of going by unnoticed – unremarked; the way, for instance, that Liz Braid said how nice it would be to have a set of tapestry kneelers for the church.

Not a ground-breaking observation at first thought, but an appeal which brought together twenty five sponsors and seventy people who promised to sew from as far afield as Portugal, New Zealand and Scotland, as well as Cobbaton and the parish itself. Four years later around 160 kneelers have been made and dedicated in a demonstration of teamwork and friendship that is more heartening, surely, than the resolution of a soap opera problem, or whether England makes it to the World Cup.

The decision to publish a book about its own parish was made at Chittlehampton without the knowledge that Halsgrove's Community Histories were already established. Patient interviewing and careful research have been rewarded with many touching, endearing, funny and fascinating stories. Goodness knows where facts may have been blurred, or dates misplaced – but it is all well intended. So it is for you who left or had to go away, as well as for those who remain, that this book is assembled and written as an affirmation and remembrance of this very beautiful small part of England's West Country.

RAE KNIGHT
EDITOR

About The Parish

by Major Peter Wood

The second half of the 19th century marked the end of the parish as a self-governing unit, being replaced by County and Rural District Councils. The Church no longer commanded the allegiance of the whole parish. All power had been given to the County and District Councils and the Parish Councils could only make representations to the higher powers.

Chittlehampton became an ecclesiastical parish in 1863 when its population was around 1,900. Eight years later it had sunk to 1,598 and by 1901 had decreased to 996. This was after allowing for the separation of Chittlehamholt in 1885. At the end of the millennium the parish now numbers about 800, including the village of Umberleigh some two miles to the west.

The parish boundary is about fifteen miles long enclosing a roughly rectangular area of about thirteen square miles. The River Taw in the west and the much smaller River Bray in the east clearly define two sides of the rectangle, and minor streams and country lanes complete the perimeter.

The land rises from west to east with the village of Chittlehampton situated on high ground almost in the middle. The land is hilly and there are several small woods. Generally small to medium fields provide a mixture of arable and grazing for cattle and sheep.

Below: *Looking up West Street in the 1890s.*

Chittlehampton

ABOUT THE PARISH

Umberleigh village, bisected by the River Taw, is spread over some 1,200 acres and has around 118 dwellings including a railway station which serves the Tarka Line between Barnstaple and Exeter. On the west bank of the river, in Atherington parish, is the Church of the Christian Fellowship as well as the Rising Sun Hotel, once very popular with salmon anglers. On the Chittlehampton side there is the railway station, Umberleigh Primary School, Murch Brothers Agricultural Engineering firm and the Gables Guesthouse. The Post Office sorts and delivers mail for seven surrounding villages. There is a quaint little timber-built Anglican church, where services are held monthly. It stands on land rented from the railway company and is called The Church of The Good Shepherd. Originally when it was built in 1873, at the expense of the parish vicar, the Reverend Trefusis, it was known as 'School Chapel'. As a place of worship it replaced the kitchen of the old farm-house at Nethercleave, where services had been held. During the week children went to school in the chapel and were taught by a Miss Selina Howard who was appointed and paid for by the vicar. The experience cannot have done her any lasting harm for she lived to the good age of 101 years.

Top: *Wooden Bridge at Umberleigh.*

Second from top: *East Street, Chittlehampton, early 1900s.*

Third from top: *West Street, 1890s.*

Bottom: *Wooden Bridge at Umberleigh.*

An amusing anecdote recounted by Prebendary John Andrews recalls how drunkeness was a problem in Trefusis' time. On his arrival in the parish Trefusis had stocked the Vicarage wine cellar in the accustomed manner, but later he became an abstainer and persuaded his parishioners to take the pledge. Apparently he went to the house of a man in the village and bought a cask of cider from him. He then opened the tap and allowed the cider to flow out of the yard and into a pigsty with the inevitable effect on the animal!

He was able to take such a liberty without too much adverse comment, but when he decided to put the choir into surplices, it was quite a different matter. There were those who left the church for the chapel.

Right: *Charlie Middleton and his cider jar, 1910.*

Below: *View of Umberleigh Bridge, 1950s.*

ABOUT THE PARISH

The Parish Church of St Hieritha in Chittlehampton makes a striking impact in this ancient Saxon village. It has, with some justification, often been referred to as 'The Cathedral of North Devon' due to the lofty tower with its complex array of elaborately carved stone pinnacles. The belfry tower was one of several in the South West formerly separated from the nave. It is not known exactly when the tower was built, but papers dated 1720 and attributed to Dean Miles in Oxford allege that the tower was designed by the same architect who designed the towers of Gloucester Cathedral and Probus Church in Cornwall. Since these towers were built in the earlier part of the 16th century, it can be assumed that the Chittlehampton tower dates from the same time. The church fills the higher side of the village Square and an avenue of lime trees forms a picturesque tunnel from the lychgate to the porch.

Early records show that the church was given in 1106 to Tewkesbury Abbey. This was the usual practice since, at the time, all churches were administered by abbeys or monasteries. When Henry VIII dissolved the monasteries, the patronage passed to John Giffard Esq. in 1572, with whose successors it remained until the end of the 17th century. In 1622 Giffard's grandson erected the monument in the north transept of the church, which is probably unique in commemorating at once five generations of his family. The Giffards were Royalist supporters during the Civil War. When it was over, the Chittlehampton parishioners petitioned Parliament, alleging that they had been miserably oppressed by Colonel Giffard. He was obliged to pay the fine of three years' net income, which amounted to £1,136. In 1762 Denys Rolle Esq. became the patron and his heirs continued up to the beginning of the 20th century.

5139.   Chittlehampton. A peep of the Church.   T.Harding Son & Co
Bath
Real Photo Serie

Suffragan

Of the many incumbents, the Reverend Robert Edward Trefusis, 1867–90, later ~~sufragen~~ Bishop of Crediton, played a major part in the church's evolution. Through his character and leadership extensive alterations and improvements to the church building were made. His successor, Albert Edward Seymour, started the *Chittlehampton Parish Magazine*. The Reverend Prebendary J H B Andrews MA became vicar in 1946 and continued in his post until his death in 1984. During his many years' service in the parish, this much-loved incumbent compiled and wrote an excellent book about Chittlehampton.

The tower was thoroughly restored in 1937 during the incumbency of Reverend Ernest Clement Mortimer at a cost of £700. The pageant of St Urith to raise funds for the restoration was more of an artistic than financial success. There are seventy two pinnacles at the top of the tower, each requiring regular and thorough maintenance.

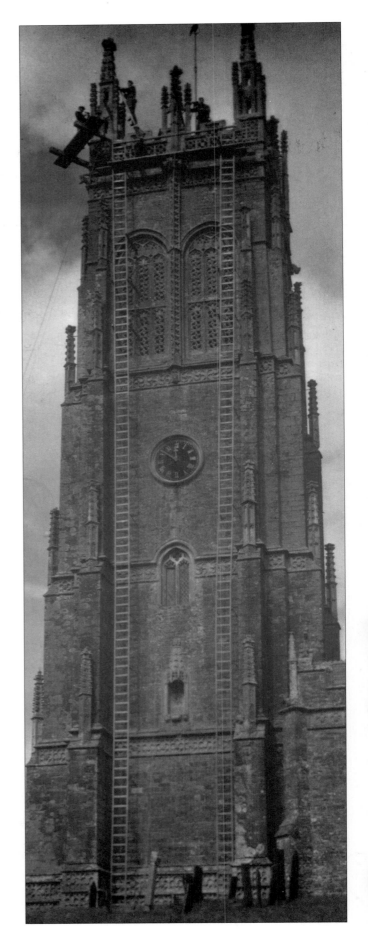

ABOUT THE PARISH

Towards the end of the 19th century a curate was considered to be a necessity for the parish. The question of where he should live was solved by converting The Green Dragon Inn, on the village main street, which was part of the glebe. This terraced, thatched cottage was renamed 'The Curatage' and was occupied by a succession of curates who lived there with their families and ponies rent free. Their stipend was paid for by Mark Rolle Esq.

The names Giffard and Rolle, lords of the manor, emerge as the most important patrons and benefactors of the church. By the beginning of the last century, the new inheritor of the trusteeship was Mark Rolle's nephew the 21st Lord Clinton (and the accession of the Rolle estate gave him a property of 70,000 acres). The excessive expenditure of his predecessor had to be curtailed and this resulted in an abrupt end to rebuilding in Chittlehampton. Another economy was the ending of the curate's stipend, which lead to the appointment of a lay reader. Lord Clinton himself supervised and became directly involved in the management of the estate. Forestry was his great interest and he was Chairman of the Forestry Commission from 1922–29.

Facing Page: *Repairing the church in 1937.*

Above: *John Giffard's family memorial.*

Right: *Giffard family tree.*

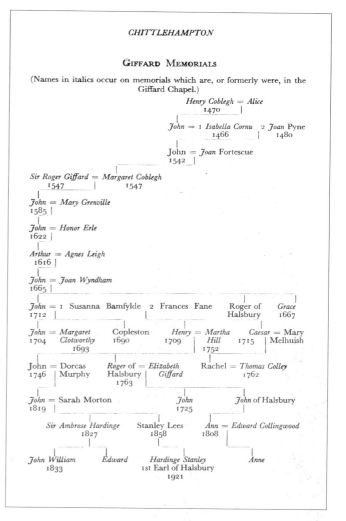

Above: *Drawing of Chittlehampton Church by W. Spreat, 1842.*

Below: *Plan of the Church of St Hieritha.*

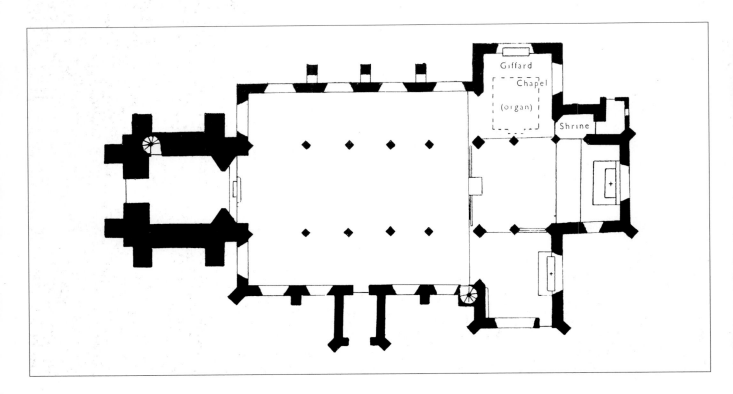

Church and Chapel

by Major Peter Wood

The church is unique in its dedication to St Hieritha, who lived and died in Chittlehampton and was buried in the church. She was believed to be a convert of St Kea of Glastonbury, who passed through North Devon in the 6th century. The legend of the saint is in the latin hymn discovered in 1901 in a 15th-century manuscript at Trinity College Cambridge. She is described as a young maiden devoted to the religious life, put to death with haymakers' scythes at the instigation of a jealous and probably heathen stepmother. Where she fell a spring of water gushed, and flowers – probably scarlet pimpernels – bloomed in the drought-ridden soil. The water was thought to have healing powers and soon pilgrims flocked to Chittlehampton to anoint their eyes with water from the well, finding their way with the help of wayside crosses.

Right: *St Tiera's Well, c.1895.*

Below: *Stone cross at Eastacott.*

©1974 Western Morning News Plymouth

Chittlehampton has always been proud of its saint. These pictures show the Pageant of St Hieritha through the sreets in 1936, 1974 and 2000.

Left: *Villagers proceed through West Street in 1974.*

Centre left: *The Reverend Mortimer and Sadie Kelly who played the young saint, 1936.*

Below: *The saint is carried to her burial.*

Bottom: *The cast of the pageant in 2000.*

©1936 Knight Photographic

©1936 Knight Photographic

©Cobbaton Photographic

Top: *Reverend Mortimer as the angel, 1936.*

Above: *The priest and villagers.*

Above right: *Scarlet Pimpernels in 1936.*
Left to right: *Rachel Parkhouse, Margaret Rendle,
Ruth Thorne, Beryl Kingdon, Pat Kelly.*

Right: *Villagers with scythes in 1936.*
Left to right, front: *Mrs Philips, Vera Mellor (née Gardiner),
Doreen Vaughn (née Gill), Hilda Kingdon (née Harris)
Peggy Carpenter (née Cole), Sadie Kelly,
Freda Clarke (née Gardiner).*

The traditional place of her martyrdom, St Urith's Well, sometimes referred to as the well of St Tiera or corrupted to Taddy's well, is at the eastern end of the village. The well was used for drinking water possibly as recently as 1880. The original structure over the well was dismantled in 1920 for reasons of safety, the area being concreted over with a manhole cover allowing access to the well. Looking inside one sees slowly flowing water and beautifully coloured unmortared stonework. A large stone which must have been the lip of the well was built into the adjacent stone wall to form a sort of sepulchre.

It seems that St Hieritha was buried near the site of her martyrdom and later a church was built over her grave, which until 1537 was the journey's end for pilgrims. In that year Henry VIII decreed that there would be no more pilgrimages. Following this decree, it is said that her remains were interred in an unmarked grave outside the church, presumably to reduce the risk of being destroyed. She was however portrayed in stone carved on the 15th-century pulpit, together with the four doctor saints, St Augustine, St Jerome, St Gregory and St Ambrose.

Pilgrims needed somewhere to stay at the end of their journey to the shrine and this probably accounts for the large number of inns in the village. At one time there were as many as eight. It is worthy of note that donations or fees paid by pilgrims to visit St Hieritha's shrine had made the benefice the wealthiest in Devon. The living was reduced from £76 a year to a mere £27 when the pilgrimages stopped. The powers of the church dwindled rapidly and, by 1540, the Abbey of Tewkesbury among others surrendered its control of the church to the crown and the last abbot became the first Bishop of Gloucester.

Having been rebuilt and enlarged in the 15th century, the church was modified again in 1872 under the direction of the incumbent, Reverend Trefusis. There were numerous changes of which the most striking was the removal of the handsome wainscot altar piece (which almost completely obscured the east window) the stripping of plaster from the internal walls and the removal of the ceiling which revealed carved ribs and bosses. Other significant changes included the lengthening of the chancel, the repositioning of the font and pulpit and the installation of a new organ in the present Giffard Chapel. Also at this time the reredos depicting the Last Supper in mosaic was installed.

As a result of the discovery of the latin hymn, mentioned earlier, interest in the saint as an historical figure was revived. The present shrine was reconstructed and the font was moved to 'the ancient usual place' near the door. In 1937 a stone figure of the saint was given to the church by Prebendary J F Chanter and fixed to the south wall of the tower about twenty feet above the base. A young girl, Sadie Kelly, who had taken part in the pageant that year, was the sculptor's model. In 1954 the Bishop of Exeter re-dedicated St Hieritha's tomb on her Feast Day.

From 1586 until 1905 the church was under the trusteeship of a group of benefactors known as feoffees. These were generally men of good standing who administered the revenue from property they owned for the benefit of the church. The last of these good men, after the death in 1905 of the Third Earl Fortescue, applied to the Charities Commission who ruled that the incumbent and the churchwardens should in future take over the duties of the feoffees.

Above: The present vicar of Chittlehampton, Revd Stephen Girling, is able to get a good view of the church's young saint during his fund-raising abseil down the church tower.

CHURCH AND CHAPEL

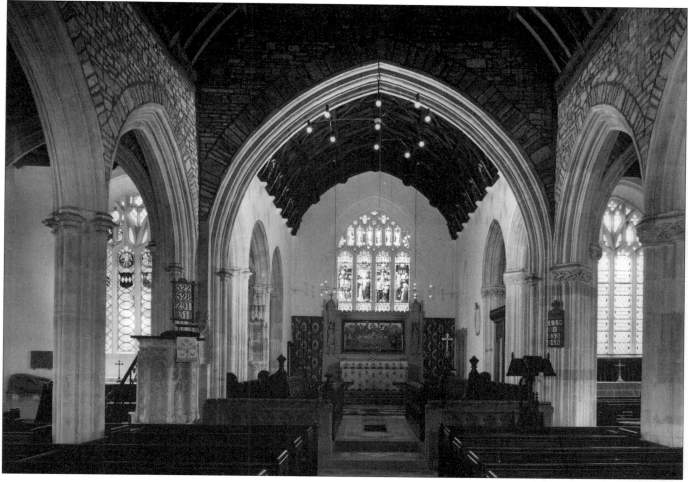

© S.W. Kenyon

Above: *Interior of the church.*

Below: *Church brass believed to be of St Hieritha.*

The churchwardens in 1721 were Arthur Nicholls and Richard Tucker and they were in trouble over the tower. They were threatened with excommunication and had to appear in court to answer charges that several pinnacles, placed as ornaments on the sides of the tower, had fallen.

On Ash Wednesday, 3 March 1897, it was recorded that:

The Parish was visited by a... severe gale... the worst mischief it did was to throw down the north east pinnacle upon the roof of the nave, crashing through it and wrecking several of the seats and injuring the flooring. Mercifully no one was in the church, though half an hour earlier a service had been held.

After only three weeks a tender from a Mr Howard for £43 to repair the roof and seats and another from a Mr Bryant for £97 to re-build the pinnacle had been accepted by the feoffees. There being only about £12 a year available for repairs, an appeal for funds from land-owners and parishioners was launched.

© Cobbaton Photographic

Again in 1990 a storm blew down two of the four tallest pinnacles. The repair work this time cost thousands of pounds which was mostly raised from public subscription. Unfortunately the repairs were less than adequate to resist the violent gales seven years later. The damage in January 1998 almost mirrored that of March 1897, but this time two pinnacles were toppled. In this latest incident the morning service had just finished and the vicar, Stephen Girling, was still in the church. The landlord of The Bell Inn, Mark Jones, saw the wobbling pinnacles and ran into the church shouting a warning. The two men dashed out just as the falling masonry came down behind them.

Below: *Two of our pinnacles are missing, 1998.*

Facing Page: *Mark Jones abseiling.*

Perhaps as evidence of gratitude for being saved as well as to raise money from sponsors for tower repairs, Stephen, one of his churchwardens Carole Henderson-Begg, and Mark Jones joined church architect Jonathan Rhind and abseiled down the tower. Carole's son Kyle also went down.

It took over six months to quantify the cost of repairing the damage, which came to about £203,000. Herbert Reid, a Tiverton-based firm of conservation and artistic builders, were contracted to reconstruct the smashed pinnacles, and their work was completed by February of 1999.

© Cobbaton Photographic

Above: *Chittlehampton bellringers of the 1920s.*

Left to right, standing: E Squire, Bert Waldron, William Webber, Jack Snow, Stan Knowles, W Dean, E J Arscott; seated: Ivan Harris, Fred Spear, Sid Rendle, Cyril Holland, Mr Mayne, Horace Waldron.

Below: *Bellringing certificate from the High Bickington Ringing Festival, 1930.*

Bellringing was an important way of keeping people in touch with major national events. As an example, financial records show that 10 shillings were given to the bellringers in 1798 for ringing on the occasion of Admiral Nelson's victory over the French fleet in the Battle of the Nile.

The ringers are a separate body and not directly under Church control. In the years succeeding the Second World War they have never failed to gain one of the six places in the county call-change competition.

The churchyard was extended to the north as recently as 1902 on land given by Mr Rolle which was being used as a garden. The cost of enclosing the extension with a stone wall was £120, and the new churchyard was consecrated by Bishop Trefusis of Crediton. In 1997 it became necessary to extend again to the north. Mr Everard Howard of Lower Biddecott Farm gave the land to the church, and it was decided to enclose it with a new stone wall. An appeal was launched to raise the £25,000 needed. Grants from the District and Parish Councils together with public subscriptions are expected to reach this figure.

An interesting illustration of fund-raising for church maintenance and improvement can be seen in records of the middle of the 18th century. Mr Denys Rolle decided to build a new pew for himself in the Lady Chapel. As a result of this, in 1740, seating throughout was replaced to match his pew at a cost of £117. At that time parishioners were obliged to pay a fixed annual rate of one penny towards the maintenance of the church. Thus the rate was then increased to nine pence per annum! These seats were '...of an unusual style, being fitted up handsomely and at considerable cost with fluted Doric pilasters and pediments.' Unfortunately, during the 1872 rebuild, these classic fittings were held to be out of place in a gothic church and were all discarded!

Below: *Bellringers of the 1980s.*
Left to right: Ron Darch, Fred Spear, Monty Bertrom, Gerald Arscott, Fred Tapp, Graham Norman, George Mayne, Aubrey Headon, Ivan Harris.

The Friendly Society, 1922.

Outside the church the most obvious reminder of Denys Rolle is the cross at Winson, an ancient cross to guide pilgrims to St Hieritha's tomb, which he restored and set up on a well-designed pedestal in 1760 and framed with trees. Perhaps surprisingly the cross bears no inscription. His successor as patron, Mark Rolle, is commemorated by a large stone cross still standing in the churchyard at Torrington.

In addition to the normal annual Christian festivals, St Hieritha's Day is celebrated on the Sunday nearest 8 July. On this occasion the choir, singing the patronal hymn, leads the congregation from the Church to St Hieritha's Well, some 300 metres down the road to the east. Prayers and an anthem are sung and all those present are invited to a blessing with water from the well.

The Male and Female Friendly Societies were each known as The Club and were on the point of closing down in 1873, when members were persuaded by the Reverend Trefusis to form a local branch of the National Deposit Friendly Society. It was funded by Lord Rolle who had bequeathed £200. In those days there was an annual celebration on Whit Tuesday, which became the one excitement

of the parochial year, when the whole parish was united.

After a church service there followed a proclamation and crowning of the village queen, then the band led the queen and the whole party to a free lunch in the Vicarage garden. In 1891 there was lunch for 200, which was followed by a cricket match in which the vicar, the Reverend Seymour, hit twenty nine out of fifty nine for the married men against the single men, who only managed eight runs! The last attempt at a Club day was in 1951 which ended with the resignation of the last secretary Mrs E H Lewis JP.

Above: Mr Norman, Revd Trefusis and Mr Burgess of The Friendly Society in 1922.

Below: An old postcard of Winson Cross.

Throughout the year there are numerous village events organised by the church including a summer fête, a barn dance and a village supper in the winter. This last has taken the form of a Burn's Night in recent years.

No history or description of the church here can be left without tribute to the Reverend Prebandery John H B Andrews. As vicar of St Hieritha's for thirty eight years, and still well remembered by the majority of the parish, it is appropriate to recall some aspects of his life and work. Although born of missionary parents in China in 1905, he lived and worked for practically his whole life in Devon, serving in the Second World War in the RNVR at sea as a chaplain and taking up his post in Chittlehampton directly after the war.

He was best known for his parochial ministry, earning an MBE for his work with the Youth Employment Service in North Devon. His wife died in 1961 and perhaps because of this loss, and having no children, he redoubled an intense interest in serving his parish. His regular historical and antiquarian notes in the monthly *Chittlehampton Chronicle* provided a wealth of information on his own and surrounding parishes.

He was a prolific writer, contributing a significant historical study of the village of Chittlehampton for The Devonshire Association.

Above: *The Hymn to St Urith.*

Left: *Reverend John Andrews.*

Below: *Chittlehampton Church Choir, 1894.*

I look upon all the world as my parish.
John Wesley (1707–1788) from his journal.

The Wesleyan Chapel in the village was built in 1858. The date over the door of the present building shows Oct 18 1905, although this is thought to be the date of renovation.

Founder members of this very important sector of the parish were John Rendle Howard, John Hunt, Philip Webber and Dick Vicary. John Richard Howard became a local preacher, travelling around the South Molton circuit on horseback from about 1890 until his death in 1930.

To those who are not familiar with the growth of the Nonconformist Church, it may come as some surprise to learn that, as late as the 1820s, Wesleyan children were excluded from the village school, and a newspaper of the time records that:

> ... *Refuge was afforded to non-conforming Ministers who were forbidden under penalty to appear within five miles of any market town... a lady at Hudscott used to entertain these non-conforming Ministers.*

The use of the word 'entertain' here must be seen as intended 'to receive hospitably, to harbour or welcome.' Later stringent clauses were brought into force forbidding any such activity.

Reference is made to the tireless work of Mrs Ethel Lewis. Daughter of the founding member John Rendle Howard, she is described as the mainstay of the chapel all her life. Affectionately known as Aunt Hett, she played the organ and ran the choir and Sunday School up to her death in October 1960.

Above: *John Rendle Howard, one of the founder members of the chapel.*

Right: *Methodist Sunday School demonstration in 1981.*

Left to right, back row: Josie Turner, Hazel Needs, Molly Thorne, Mary Burgess, Mrs Parker, Ian Meridith, Joanna Baxter;

middle row: Clifford Needs, Martin Davis, Lee Meridith, Richard Crocker, Kevin Waldron, Philip Turner, Rowena Baxter, Pat Davis, Vicky Slape, Phil Lewis;

front row: Mark Crocker, Hannah Turner, Lucy Isaac, Lisa Meridith, Emma Turner, Juliet Waldron, Sharon Howard, Brett Meridith.

Above: *A celebration at Chittlehampton Chapel, 1889.*

The chapel was first licensed for weddings in 1894 The *North Devon Journal* reported in its edition of 25 September 1894:

The first marriage in the Wesleyan Chapel was celebrated on Wednesday of last week when the Reverend H Cotton joined together in bonds of matrimony Mr Joshua Prout and Miss Emily Lewis.

Mr Prout's parents gave the communion rail to the chapel and Emily Prout's sister, Mrs Alice Buckingham, donated the communion table in memory of Emily.

The chapel was renovated in 1889, though by then the choir no longer existed and now, as with so many other denominations, the chapel records with sadness that the once strong and flourishing congregation is dwindling.

Beware you be not swallowed up in books! An ounce of love is worth a pound of knowledge.
                                Life of Wesley, 1820

Top: *Chittlehampton Methodist Church Choir, 1894.*

Left to right, standing: Ned Southcombe, Jim Cole, Dick Vicary, Ned Sanders, Carter Watts, Jim Lewis, Jim Towell, John Huxtable;

centre row: Bob Snow, Mrs William Mayne, Mrs Sarah Mules, Mrs Amelia Howard, Miss Emily Lewis, Miss Ethel Howard, Mrs Maud Cole, Sam Towell;

front row: Annie Huxtable, Ada Towell, Selomie Cole, Nellie Davis, Jenny Webber.

Above: *Group assembled for the marriage of Harold Davey and Hilda Howard.*

Thought For The Day

What is the Church anyway? The inherited, traditional model of the Anglican Church in this parish invested a lot in the priest and the church building. 'It's my church' has often meant 'The church building that I love'. 'Nobody ever visits me from the church' often meant 'The vicar hasn't called'. But the church was never meant to be the building or the priest – it is organic, it is the people who's faith in Christ draws them together in love for worship, growth and mission.

I am a parish priest serving Chittlehampton and the parish of Filleigh, a combined population of 1100. With a diminishing number of paid parish priests in the Church of England, the Diocese of Exeter, of which we are a part, reckons on rural priests serving 2000 or more people and urban priests around 7000 or more. For those in our community who consider the priest to be 'the Church' this is a cause for alarm, because clearly the 'slice of priest' available for each community will continue to diminish in the future. Furthermore, as the cost of maintaining church buildings continues to escalate as they get older, for those who consider the building to be 'the Church' this too is a cause for alarm.

However, I strongly believe we should not be alarmed! A priest is called to represent people to God and to represent God to people. In that respect any committed Christian can be a priest. It is exciting to see how increasing numbers of local committed Christians are involved in visiting, in leading prayers and worship, and in teaching. Even without a paid priest and without a building, the Church would still be here – because the Church is the gathered community of faith, of whatever denomination, wherever they gather and whoever gathers them!

One of the things I love about this community is the sense of near 'timelessness', the feeling that in North Devon we can shield or isolate ourselves from those things in the rest of society that we don't like or wouldn't like for our children. It's as if we are happy being just one step behind society; when it suits us to catch up we'll do so in our own way and time.

As we face the 21st century, our community needs to recognise how the Church too is changing in a rapidly changing world, sometimes swimming with the tide, sometimes against it. Some would see the Church as the guardian of values, traditions and practises which can give stability in an ever-changing world. To some extent that is true; for example the church particularly values the role it plays in our two village schools, in bringing the community together for festivals and special occasions, and in serving the community at times of great joy or great sorrow. However, the Church is not called upon to be a guardian of the past kept in a cabinet for people to enjoy when it suits them, the Church is called upon to be a living, changing and vibrant part of the community, distinct but not separate.

It's my belief as parish priest that as the Church continues to serve and be served by our community we are in the process of becoming leaner and fitter, less archaic and more relevant, less introspective and more outward looking – truly 'Reaching Upwards and Outwards'. This is not the Church in survival mode, this is the Church renewing itself. May God continue to favour us in this beautiful, spacious place.

THE REVEREND STEPHEN GIRLING, BA, BSc
VICAR OF ST HIERITHA'S CHURCH,
CHITTLEHAMPTON

A 16th-century map of Britian found in Italy on which Chittlehampton is marked.

Above: *Barbara Neville, Stella Levy, and Liz and Mike Braid with Chittlehampton's prayer kneelers.*

Below: *Clinton Estate Land Sale Map, 1958.*

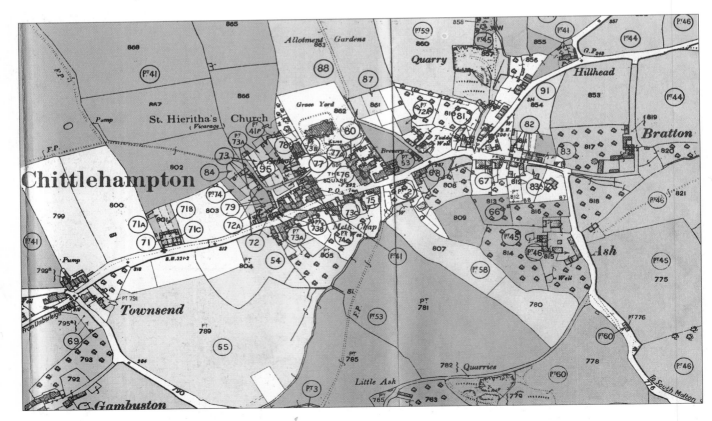

Some Historic Houses

by Major Peter Wood

An unusually long weir at Umberleigh divides the parishes of Atherington and Chittlehampton. It separates the mill, which was in the manor of Umberleigh, from the two sluices, which were in the manor of Brightley, and so could render the mill useless.

Above: *Fishing at Brightley Weir in the early 1900s.*

Below: *John Thomas at Brightley Barton, 2000.*

The lords of these two manors were not always on good terms and there were frequent disputes over fish (salmon and sea trout) and the availability of sufficient water for the mill. Unusually there appeared to be no record of marriages between the two families which successively owned them, despite the general truth of Dr Johnson's observation that 'proximity makes marriages'. It is said that the weir was the crossing point used by Royalist troops of Colonel John Giffard of Brightley during the Civil War.

Several hundred years ago it was the custom to give eminent people land as reward for their services to the Crown. They built fine houses which usually had farm buildings attached and dwellings for the farm hands. In North Devon at least such a complex was know as a 'barton'. This word is said to derive from the Old English 'beer-tun' meaning a barley enclosure, and is defined as a demesne farm, that is, the land which the owner kept in hand for his own living.

Some time in the 12th century, William Fitzwarren inherited the property known now as Brightley Barton. The cob-built house was surrounded by a moat (which still remains) to keep wild beasts out and domestic animals in. In the middle of the 14th century, Roger Giffard, a descendent of Walter Giffard who was related to Edward the Confessor, married the daughter of John Cobleigh of Brightley, one of the richest heiresses in Devon

In due course Giffard inherited Brightley Barton and made the grounds into a park. The name Park Gate, where there is now a group of houses and the great trees nearby, are all that remain of this park, and of Sir Roger's house one room only survives, incorporated in the present building. The crest over the front door relates to the Fitzwarrens, the Cobleighs and the Giffards. It is hard to picture it, as it must have been one of the great houses of North Devon, affording quarters during the Civil War for 300 Royalist troops. In 1737 Samuel Rolle bought Brightley Barton from the executors of Caesar Giffard.

Later in the 19th century the plaque on the south wall of the church dedicated to a certain John Nicholls at Brightley added further interest. Towards the end of the same century the Reverend Mortimer, vicar of the parish, was also resident at Brightley.

Above: *The crest at Brightley Barton.*

Below: *Hawkridge House, 1933.*

Hawkridge Barton is another example of an important house in the parish which until 1998 was a flourishing farm on the Chichester Estate. Although still part of that estate it is now a family home rather than a farm. In his book *Worthies of Devon* (1701) the Devon historian Prince wrote about Baldwin Acland, owner of Hawkridge:

He was descended from the family of Acland that long flourished at Hawkridge in the parish of Chittlehampton, whose church has been notable for the interment there of a famous saint, Hieritha by name.

The arms of a Baldwin Acland, who died in 1659, were set up over the fireplace and remain there to this day.

Above: *The Acland coat of arms over the fireplace at Hawkridge.*

Below: *Hudscott Manor.*

Another large and very old house in the parish is Hudscott, which was first mentioned in an Assize Roll of 1281. The name Hudscott probably stems from its Saxon tenant, Hudda. It was one of the ten ancient free tenements of the Manor of Chittlehampton. The tenants of a free tenement paid only a small chief-rent each year. In the case of Hudscott in 1281 that was 6½d. In the mid-17th century a John Lovering was the tenant. He had married the daughter of John Dodderidge, an MP for Barnstaple. The overmantle at Hudscott has the arms of Lovering and Dodderidge and much of the present house is of the same date. Lovering's only surviving child, Jane, married Samuel Rolle in 1700 and Hudscott thus passed to the Rolle family. Around this time a charming clock pavilion was built in the grounds of the house, which still retains the date (February 1711) and the name of its famous maker – Lewes Pridham of Sandford. It is the oldest working clockhouse in Devon. Hudscott has been referred to as a manor. This was probably not a formal title, but may have been used in connection with the house being the residence of 'the lord of the manor' for nearly three centuries.

Bradbury Barton is the last of the four 'bartons' in the parish. It is mentioned in the Domesday Book where the name Bradbury was then 'Braia'. It has never been sold, but descended from the heiress of Nicholas de Fileleye in the 13th century. It belongs to the Fortescue Estate of Castle Hill in the neighbouring parish. There are no records of this house ever being occupied by an eminent person. However, it was and still is important for its demesne land which in 1842 extended to 223 acres.

Another old house on the outskirts of the village is known as 'Court'. Its name stems from its former role as the house where the manor courts were held.

Only two 'rolls' for the manor court survive to this day. The one for 1537 bears examination as an insight into the nature of rural crime pertaining in the parish of Chittlehampton in the reign of Henry VIII. The Marquis of Exeter was lord of the manor at that time. The court roll states that there were 12 jurors, who had to deliberate on a variety of different cases. One of these concerned the disposal of three lambs, a ram and two sheep, which had strayed. They were sold according to the custom. The records don't say who benefited from the sale, which realised 2s.6d.

Other cases dealt with unpaid debts and petitions for annual licences to brew ale by seven applicants, each of whom paid 4d. for the right to tap and sell ale.

There seem to have been cases of breaches of the peace, in one of which a certain Henry Pitt attacked and injured one John Dun with a stick. His fine was 9d. The said John Dun was fined 4d. for attacking Henry Pitt with a stick. The rolls do not explain whether the incidents were separate or if a plea of self defence was offered. Perhaps society in those days was not so 'blessed' with the plethora of lawyers advocating litigation to the same extent as today.

Below: *The clock pavilion at Hudscott.*

The decision of the Clinton Devon Estate to dispose of most of their North Devon property in 1958 came as a shock to most of the tenants. The estate intended to sell some 3,000 acres in the parish. The change dreaded by some at first could be seen as an advantage in future times of prosperity. There were many who would have preferred to continue as tenants.

This sale was on such a large scale that a major national monthly magazine, *Country Life*, carried a full-page advertisement of the impending sale of over 15,000 acres of the Clinton Estate, which at that time was producing a rental of some £28,000. There were illustrations of Hudscott, Brightley Barton and the Biddacotts.

The sale took place over several months, during which time individual tenants negotiated their purchases by private treaty with the Clinton Estate. The end result was a significant break with the past in Chittlehampton. A titled land-owner had thus formally ended his ties with the parish and the villagers were now severally the new land-owners. There were no previous records of the sale of Hudscott, which had been inherited by the Rolle family in the 18th century. Brightley Barton, which included some 1,300 acres, had been sold previously in 1737 for £9,550 to Samuel Rolle, by the representatives of Caesar Giffard. Between 1737 and 1957 there had been only five owners, all descendents of the Rolle family. Without exception they had been of great benefit to the parish.

Farming

Chittlehampton Young Farmers' Club

© Knight Photographic

If the youth of a village is healthy and energetic, there is usually not much wrong with the rest of the parish.

The fifty two members of CYFC won best Club in Devon in 1997–8. Their activities when described seem more appropriate to a Club three times the size, and they take on worthy challenges like raising £5,200 for charity.

They certainly know how to have fun. Who could forget their version of The Full Monty performed at the parish pantomime?

You have to be between ten and twenty six years old to be a member, and the activities are divided between fund-raising, educational, entertainment and sporting projects. They particularly enjoy exchange visits throughout the country.

© Express & Echo

© North Devon Journal

Top left: *YFC Field Day, mid 1950s.*

Left to right: Wilfred Harris, Albert Cook, Mary Arscott, Margaret Burgess, John Hosking, Harold Sussex, Betty Burgess.

Top right: *Peter Gill, George Harris and Vera Huxtable.*

Centre: *Gerald Arscott, Myrtle Arscott, Jack Carter (Mayor of South Molton) and George Harris.*

Left: *Chittlehampton YFC in 1998 – the best in Devon.*

The Changing Scenes of Agriculture in the 20th Century

by John Hosking

My memories go back to the early years of the Second World War when the horse gave way to the tractor. This period was preceded by the Great Depression of the thirties so the transformation of agriculture was greatly emphasised by the need to produce all the food we could, because our merchant shipping was being threatened by German U-Boats.

I remember when our new Fordson tractor arrived in 1941. The front wheels were iron with a raised rib in the middle to enable us to steer. The rear wheels were also metal and smooth, to which we had to bolt two rows of triangular lumps of iron ('spade-lugs' as they were called). These were placed alternately on the edges of the wheel as grips. Of course the tractor was no use on its own, so new implements had to be purchased or adapted.

FARMING

I remember Murch Bros. making iron frames to bolt on to the shafts of long-tailed carts. This was a great help at harvest time when so much more corn had to be grown. The Government had decreed that farmers must plough a third of their holdings to grow corn or potatoes (we could hire sacks for corn and they provided sacks for potatoes).

The 1947 Agricultural Act brought more stability to farming by introducing guaranteed prices which were negotiated between the Government and the National Farmers Union. This provided that if a product failed to make the agreed standard price the Government would make up the deficiency. These reforms helped to maintain higher food production and to increase the mechanisation of farming, but of course led to the gradual demise of many of the rural crafts.

As a boy, one of the things I looked forward to was threshing. There were no sheds in those days and all the corn was collected in ricks (which were thatched immediately after harvest). The ricks were made near the gateway of the field so that the traction engine pulling the thresher didn't have to go far into the field, as they often bogged down in a wet period.

Two enginemen would arrive at the farm at seven o'clock to light the boiler to get up steam. Breakfast was to be ready at eight o'clock (the farmer's wife was expected to provide this). She also had to prepare lunch and sometimes tea for thirteen or fourteen men, the usual number for a threshing team. The men were neighbouring farmers or their workmen.

Facing page above: *Wilf Harris ploughing at Whey Farm, 1950s.*

Facing page below: *Harvesting time, 1940. Mr Munn is standing on the left and Bill Stone is on the cart.*

Top: *Burrell Traction engines at West Buckland, 1930s.*

Above: *'Pride of the West' No: 3739 Reg No: AF3836, built in 1916 and owned by A H Murch, photographed at Dorridge in 1950.*

Left: *Bert Phillips.*

Above: *Murch reedcomber and crew, early 1970s.*

Left to right: Michael Hosking, Harry Murch, John Smith, Fred Spear, Arthur Philips, Reg Buckingham, Tom Thorne, Peter Tucker, John Thorne, Arthur Squires, Tony Smith, Michael Buckingham, Gerald Arscott, Ernie Smith, Jimmy Woolacott.

Left: *Kenneth Waldon, c.1940.*

Below: *Combine harvester, 1950s. Harry Murch and Charlie Stone are on the Murch's combine with George Peters in the background.*

Facing page: *Fred Spear on the left tying the reed with Harry Murch and Ern Smith inspecting the reed.*

In 1957 we hired a combine harvester from Mr Andrew of Umberleigh Barton (the first farmer to purchase one locally) and that of course was the beginning of the end of the threshing-drum.

About this time another machine began to emerge which would eventually transform the appearance of the countryside: the hedge trimmer. These early models were cumbersome, bolted on to a tractor-drawn trailer and driven by a small petrol engine. They were operated manually and worked on a swivel which was in a horizontal position so could only be used for 'topping'. I can well remember my father driving the tractor while I strove to guide the cutter accurately. Thank goodness there were no health and safety officers around in those days!

It is worth explaining here the importance of hedge maintenance. Up to this period (late 1940s) nearly all farmhouses and cottages had open fireplaces which consumed vast quantities of wood. It was the practice on most farms to 'make' two or three hedges every winter which entailed making up the banks and layering the saplings horizontally along the top, so that the more mature wood could be used for fuel.

©Tony Freeman Press Agency

Above: *Bill Rodd at Murch Bros., fifty years a wheelright!*

Above right: *Left to right, back row: Brian Stuckey, Brian Thorne, Joe Hedges, Dennis Huxtable, Brian Alford, George Stuckey, Ivan Huxtable;*
front row: Art Phillips, Sam Heale, Fred Saunders, Lionel Phillips, Malcolm Vile, Dan Murch, Bob Westcott, Pat Murch.

Below: *The Murch's traction engine, before the Second World War, with Lloyd Murch on the left and Harry Murch on the right.*

Above: *Murch Bros., 1970s.*

Left to right on tractors: Tony Folland, Bev Huxtable, Pat Murch, George Stuckey, Jim Edwards, Bob Westacott, Johnny Seterton, Ray Congram, Ernie Summerville, Fred Sanders, Bill Ford; standing: Frank Stuckey, Dan Murch.

Below: *A H Murch and young Barry Murch.*

However, from this period onwards we saw a gradual increase in modern stoves and fireplaces in our farmhouses which would require much less wood as fuel, and with the end of the war came the increased availability of coal. The continual need for food production and increasing mechanisation meant that farmers now regarded hedges around small fields as a hindrance and liability. This led to the removal of thousands of miles of hedgerows, a practice which continued until the late 1900s (it is now an offence to remove a hedge without planning permission). Fortunately, our own parish, being largely a livestock area, has retained reasonably small fields compared with the mainly arable areas of Southern and Eastern England.

The year 1958 was an important one for many farmers in the parish for it saw the sale of the northern section of Clinton Estates. The majority of the farmland and a large part of the village was owned by Lord Clinton. Most tenants were offered the chance to purchase their farms (at approximately £40 per acre), and most accepted. Today when farmland changes hands at approximately £2,000 per acre it is hard to believe that many tenants had difficulty in raising enough capital to purchase their farms. It was the changing economic climate in the following decades that brought about the transition of a way of life into the agri-business that farming has become today.

The post-war years saw the introduction of newer breeds of sheep and cattle, especially in the dairy sector. The dairy Shorthorns, Channel Island breeds and Ayrshires were being replaced by the British Dutch Friesians.

By the 1970s the national herd was almost entirely black and white, as it is today, although many have been crossed with Canadian Holstein. In the beef sector our native North Devons have almost come into rare-breed category. Our fields now contain beef cattle of all shades resulting from crossing Friesian cows with Continental bulls.

Our dear old Devon Closewool sheep have also nearly disappeared, having been largely replaced by various breeds from other parts of the country and abroad which produce twice as many lambs. Our arable crops now produce twice or even three times as much as they did fifty years ago as a result of modern science and technology.

Above: *Mr Bulled with a Closewool champion ram.*

Below: *Johnathon Waterer and Shires, Higher Biddacott Farm, 1999.*

© Bernard Chambers

FARMING

The weather has always been an important facet of our daily lives. It affects all of us directly or indirectly, especially now when the temperature is rising worldwide. Most of our parish boundaries are in fact substandard water courses. Hawkridge Brook forms a large part of the northern boundary, the River Bray part of the eastern and southern boundaries and the River Taw the long boundary of the south western end of the parish. Flooding is a major concern for farmers and householders who live near these rivers.

October 1960 was probably one of the wettest ever recorded (19 inches on Exmoor). South Devon had the severest flooding, but the River Taw broke its banks on four occasions, flooding houses in Umberleigh. This very wet autumn came to a climax on Sunday 4 December. Early on Saturday four inches of rain fell over the whole catchment area of the Taw and its main tributaries, the Bray and Mole.

© Victor Harris

This exceptional rainfall on the already saturated land caused the river to rise to the highest level for 150 years. Houses at Umberleigh were flooded to a depth of twenty eight inches. Murch Bros., the Post Office and many other properties were also flooded.

Eight years later, in January 1968, the peak of the flood was only a few inches lower than that of 1960 but most people were more prepared and less damage occurred, although over 300 sheep were lost in the Taw Valley. This was in part caused by the restrictions on the movement of animals at the time because of a local outbreak of foot and mouth disease. Farmers simply didn't have time to obtain the necessary permission to move them.

Above: The flood at Umberleigh, Friday 30 September 1960.

Right: Barry Murch clearing snow in February 1978.

The next serious flood came thirty six years later in October 1998. The peak was fifteen inches lower than the flood of 1960.

Although the winters of 1947 and 1963 are regarded as having been the coldest of the 20th century there is no doubt that the blizzard of 17 February 1978 was the worst since 1891.

The winter of that year had been quite mild until the second week of February when rain was forecast. Indeed it did begin to rain on Valentine's Day but turned to sleet and then snow in the evening. The next day was Thursday and we had another slight fall. Friday was quiet but dry. Saturday dawned cloudy and very cold with an increasing south-easterly wind. By midday it had reached gale force and the snow was drifting (hedge high in places). By mid-afternoon it was snowing heavily and by evening virtually all roads were impassable.

Snow continued all through the night and until the middle of Sunday morning. Every road that ran north–south was full of snow. Hundreds of sheep were buried and even some buildings. For the next three days hardly anything moved, no cars or trains, just a few tractors. It was so quiet that a local newspaper described North Devon as a cemetery.

Thousands of gallons of milk were lost because the tankers could not move. This was the first time that milk tankers had encountered snow since the switchover from churn lorries and the drivers were unprepared for the chaos that ensued. Helicopters played a big part in the crisis, dropping food to isolated homes and fodder for the animals. It was estimated that 3,500 sheep died in the snow; nearly every sheep farmer in the parish lost a few and some lost many. It is said that it took eighty machines three weeks to clear the roads in North Devon after that blizzard.

THE BOOK OF CHITTLEHAMPTON

So where does farming in Chittlehampton go from here? During the last sixty years there have been more changes in every aspect of farming than in the last 600. The outlook for the future has never been more uncertain than at present. The prospect of a single currency for most of Europe, the phasing out of subsidies which have sustained our farms for the last fifty years and the controversies over genetic engineering, global warming and environmental restrictions all tend to make farming a daunting challenge in the immediate future, but hasn't it always been the same? I think that there will be a tendency towards larger farms and, paradoxically, more part-time or 'hobby farmers' in the future.

And what of 'our native North Devons'? Also known as Red Devons, these wonderful, sturdy cattle are quite distinct from the South Devons, and although becoming rare, can certainly still be seen. One of the most distinguished breeders in North Devon is John Thomas of Brightley Barton. His contribution here speaks for itself:

Devon cattle have taken pride of place in livestock at Brightley Barton for seventy years. They have featured in many agricultural shows throughout the United Kingdom. Many have been exported to Australia, South America and South Africa. Their ability to forage on shrub and heathland has made them extremely popular in these countries. It has been a privilege to have been invited to judge cattle at the Royal Show in Perth, Western Australia, and the Royal Show in Porte Alegre in Brazil. Numbered amongst my own successes have been two championships at Royal Smithfield and a commendation for the breed at the Royal Show Championships.

Left: *John Thomas judging a Devon Ruby Red at the County Show.*

Below: *A delegation from New Zealand at Brightley Barton inspect the Devon Reds.*

© Knights Photographic

FARMING

A New Enterprise at Langaton

by Ian Waldon

Lower Langaton was originally farmed by my great-grandfather Jones in the early 1900s. The farm was tenanted from the Clinton Estate and consisted of 125 acres of mixed farming employing six men.

I learned that my great-grandfather committed suicide during the Depression years. I understand that he lost a lot of money during the Stock Market crash which obviously affected him badly. My grandfather Horace Waldron, who had married my great-grandfather's daughter, Irene Jones, took on the farm and ran it until my father and mother in turn took over in April 1959 – one month before I was born. They bought it in 1958 for £6,000 from the Clinton Estate.

My father farmed dairy and sheep until 1972 when he sold our forty-five-cow dairy herd in order to concentrate on sheep. I left school in 1975 and came home to work on the farm. I began my own pig herd, keeping up to twenty five sows, Welsh and Large Whites; they produced weaners which I sold to be finished. I also carried out some casual work for local farmers.

In 1978 we decided to return to the dairy industry, investing in sixty cows and at the same time reducing the sheep numbers.

My father died in 1981 following a very short illness, so I was then responsible for running the farm at the age of twenty two, together with my mother. Following my father's death I decided to give up my pig herd and the sheep in order to concentrate on cows which at that time were consistently profitable. Through the 1980s into the '90s we managed to purchase land – expanding to 177 acres and increasing the dairy herd to 105. In 1994 I married Rachel Hunt.

Late in 1995 we read an article about alpaca farming which interested us since the state of agriculture was then becoming more and more depressing. Farming alpacas involves no slaughtering. They are kept purely for the wool which is three times stronger than sheep wool but much softer and highly sought after in an under-supplied market. These advantages, combined with apparent ease of management, convinced us that it had to be worth diversifying. At that time there were only 600 alpacas in the UK and less than three million in the world, which meant an opportunity to sell breeding stock for some years to come.

In October 1996 we bought our first two pregnant alpacas. These births and further purchases have brought our herd to approaching forty females. We are now concentrating on breeding quality stock to sell on as nucleus stock to other breeders, with the returns from the wool becoming more important as the national herd increases.

We are so encouraged by growth in the alpaca industry that we have disposed of our dairy herd in order to concentrate on this new enterprise.

The wool from alpacas is pooled nationally by a co-op, which was formed by breeders in 1998, and graded and manufactured into the end product which in turn is marketed in top UK stores such as Harrods.

On the family front we now have two daughters, Daisy and Tabitha; you never know, one of them may be interested one day in high-fashion knitwear or farming alpacas.

© Cobbaton Photographic

Left: *Alpacas at Langaton.*

THE BOOK OF CHITTLEHAMPTON

The diary of C W Stone of Higher Biddacott Farm

These notes of a farmer from the early part of the last century tell a rich tale of farming in North Devon in those years.

12 February 1926	*Went to Barnstaple to order manure distributor – £16.10s.*
14 September 1926	*Sold two rams at Umberleigh – Two teeth @ 6.³/₄ guineas. Six teeth @ 4.³/₄ guineas*
10 October 1926	*Lloyd George came to Barnstaple.*
24 November 1926	*School children played football at High Bickington. Three goals each.*
14 December 1926	*Umberleigh Auction, sold ten hogs @ 45/- each*
22 December 1926	*Barnstaple Xmas market Turkeys 2/-, 2/2d., 2/6d. lb. Butter 2/4d. per lb.*
23 January 1932	*Chittlehampton F.C. played Tiverton. Lost 12 - 1.*
14 March 1932	*Went to Hawkridge sale.*
21 May 1932	*Chittlehampton played Kings Nympton. Won 7 - 1.*
3 October 1932	*Foot and mouth disease broke out at Combe Martin.*
22 December 1932	*Barnstaple Xmas market. Butter 1/7d. per lb., Eggs 1/7d.*
	Turkeys 1/10d., 2/- and chickens 1/4d. per lb.
13 June 1940	*We had two little girls from London through the evacuation scheme*
	for the duration of the war.
4 May 1941	*Very frosty this morning, ice about.*
	Put the clocks over two hours in front of the sun.
1 June 1941	*Jim Skinner's house (Brimley) burnt to the ground this afternoon.*
3 August 1942	*Garden Show for the Red Cross in the schoolroom.*
30 June 1946	*Rev. Andrew's first Sunday at the church.*
8 February 1947	*The whole of England covered with snow.*
13 April 1947	*Change to double summer time.*
25 June 1947	*Women's Institute outing to Dartmouth.*
22 May 1948	*Chittlehampton played football at Bickington. Lost.*
10 October 1948	*Memorial service at the church. Lord Fortescue unveiled the memorial.*
14 July 1951	*Lady Clinton laid foundation stone for the Village Hall.*
12 May 1953	*Devon County Show at South Molton. Fine day.*
2 June 1953	*Coronation of Queen Elizabeth II. Rather cold.*
	Had a bonfire in Strangs field. Sports in Abbots Hill

© Knights Photographic

Farming – A Look Ahead

by Maurice Jones

The structure of farming in the new millennium will be strongly influenced by the European Union and its Common Agricultural Policy (CAP). This in turn is influenced by the World Trade Organisation and the drive towards a global pricing structure for agricultural products. This seems a long way from rural North Devon, but with near-instantaneous communications and sophisticated transport networks, agricultural prices are being determined increasingly by fewer and fewer large purchasers with the ability to influence prices to their advantage.

The Government's strategy for agriculture is threefold:

* Farms must become more efficient to be competitive in the global market (ie become bigger)

* Smaller family farms, in particular, must diversify to obtain alternative sources of income.

* Financial support under the CAP will increasingly move from commodities to agri-environmental schemes.

Within the North Devon area much of this transition has started, being forced by the large number of relatively small family farms. Many farmhouses have been sold with a few acres for residential purposes and the bulk of the land being assimilated into neighbouring farms; this has happened with private, council and estate farms within the parish. With larger herds and flocks more advantage can be taken of modern technology to increase efficiency, albeit mainly at the expense of employed labour. However, the nature of the local terrain and land quality does not lend itself to large ranch-style farming, or to major arable crops and so there is a limit to what can be achieved in this area.

There is a history of diversification in local farming. The tourist industry is already being catered for with B&B and holiday lettings, and the last few years have shown major increases in this area. Many farmers have supplemented their farm income by contract work and this is likely to increase with less permanent on-farm employment.

The scope for limited agricultural machinery manufacture and repair is already being addressed together with alternative stock such as deer and alpacas. An area still to be exploited is the advent of farmers' markets, which used to be a regular feature in North Devon only to disappear and be re-invented by the Americans. These markets provide an opportunity for farmers to sell direct to the customer and in this respect there is also scope for farm shops which are starting to appear locally. There is increasing interest in the purchase of local food produced under welfare-friendly conditions with a minimum of additives.

The possibilities for agri-environmental schemes is only beginning to be addressed, although the CAP concentration on such schemes should ensure that they will assume a high priority. The lack of a comprehensive footpath structure within the parish limits participation to some extent but the preservation of the small family farm should provide opportunities for some limited schemes.

Within the parish of Chittlehampton the structure of farming is already being geared to the new millennium with larger, more efficient farms being developed. Alternative sources of income are being exploited but the scope for agri-environmental schemes remains limited to some extent by the terrain and the physical structure of the local farming environment.

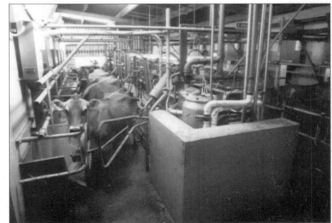

© Cobbaton Photographic

Above: *Modern milking parlour at Great Blakewell Farm.*

Facing Page: *Lady Clinton lays the Village Hall foundation stone. The flowers were presented by Ruth Stone.*

FARMING

Facing page above left: *Harvest time at Higher Biddacott, 1940. Charlie and Bill Stone are on top of the cornstack, standing are Mr Munn, Dick and Lillian Wythe and children from the village.*

Facing page below left: *Potato planting at Deptford Farm, 1957/8. Barry Murch, Ern Tapscott and Pat Murch are planting, Jimmy Ruston is driving.*

Facing page above right: *Mr and Mrs Boucher at Southcott, Brightley, milking the goat, 1960s.*

Facing page above centre right: *Harvesters in, 1940.*
Left to right: Ern Squires, Charlie Stone, Mr Munn, Bill Stone;
sitting: Dick Wythe, Carlo the dog, Frank Squires.

Facing page below centre right: *Alice Stone plucking a duck whilst Pam Francis looks on, late 1940s.*

Facing page below right: *Charlie Stone with his milk churn carrier, 1930s.*

Above: *Bill Stone and Percy Snell in the late 1930s.*

Above right: *Murch Bros. reedcomber.*

Centre right: *Frank Squires with 'Farmer' at Higher Biddacott, 1940s.*

Below right: *Victor Harris collecting eggs in the early 1950s.*

Below: *Penelope Nott at Collacott Farm.*

Memories of Shops and Businesses

by Roger Cockram

The story of a village can often be seen best through the lives of its inhabitants; where they live, where they work, where they play, where they worship, what they do. This contribution is intended to catch a glimpse of the changes that have occurred in Chittlehampton through the activities of the people who have run, or are still running, the small businesses and shops here.

A number of people have kindly offered to look back on this aspect of village life at a particular period in time. They have taken, as it were, 'a walk through the village' and tried to recall, often with great success and in some detail, the shops, the shopkeepers and the people who represented the commercial life of the village. This is not intended to be a dry history, but rather a lively testament of some of the villagers of today, calling up life in the parish in times past, and up to the year 2000.

Each person has tried to remember a particular period, even a particular year, so as to give us a real sense of the changes that have taken place between then and now.

We begin with Lilian Wythe, a lady who was born at Cobbaton, one mile north of Chittlehampton in 1920. 'The village was certainly a very different place then, m'dear'.

Chittlehampton was still part of the huge Rolle/ Clinton estate with most houses and farms rented, of course. Although great changes had been forced on the community as a result of the Great War, the area still had many of the characteristics of 19th-century England. In those days the county was only just beginning the huge changes associated with mechanisation (both of transport and of agriculture) and most villages in Devon were still, in large measure, self-sufficient, with many items for everyday existence being obtained from within the community.

Above: *The smithy.*

Right: *Harry Potter, blacksmith.*

Facing page: *Taking the bull along West Street to the butchers, 1920s.*

Lilian walked from Cobbaton to the village school in Chittlehampton from the age of five, and moved to the village (Myrtle Cottage, on the road to Cobbaton) at the age of eight. She walked through the village every day until she left school at fifteen to work in service for Colonel Smith at Stowford for five years, at which time she married husband Dick.

Lilian's 'walk through the village' starts in 1935 at Hillhead. She remembers a Mrs Baker at the house next to the forge. This lady sold wallpaper, paints, crockery, sponge-tins etc., also paint and paraffin, in fact 'wotever you couldn' get nowhere else'.

At the bottom of Hillhead, Mr Vickery ran the forge, with Harry Potter as his apprentice. Lilian says they shod horses 'from the village and for miles around'.

The bakery at East Street was run by the Lewis family, and we'll hear about the famous crunchy biscuits later. At the bottom of the Square, the Post Office was run by another Mr Lewis – Jim, this time. He sold tablecloths, wool, paper and stationery. Lilian remembers that he lived next door in Wyndhams, which he also ran as a Friendly Society. She remembers too that he would close up and walk round the village to deliver a 'telegraph' (telegram). How times change!

The pub at that time was run by Mr William H Locke. Lilian remembers going into the 'cubby-hole' (off-sales?) and having to stand on tiptoe to speak to whoever was serving.

At the lower western corner of the Square there was a shop (Corner Cottage) owned in 1935 by Mr George Mules, who was assisted by his daughter Miss Mules. This lady, according to later accounts, was something of a 'character'. Mr Mules was a tailor but Lilian can remember going there for 'a pen'orth of sweets as well'.

Lilian remembers a saddler – Mr Brayley – living and working in Barley Mow Cottage, opposite the present shop where, at that time, Mrs Gill sold groceries, cigarettes and tobacco.

Left: *Mrs Phillips outside Barley Mo papershop formerly a 19th-century inn.*

Above: *J R Burgess and Alice Stone behind the original butcher's shop, early 1920s.*

Next door was a butcher's shop, run by Mr Burgess (grandfather of Gordon Burgess who later ran the butcher's shop at Greenfields) – 'An' 'e killed the animals out back, too!'

On her daily walk through the village, Lilian would pass the tennis court where Mayflower Close is now and then arrive at the last cluster of businesses at Townsend. Townsend House had been a coaching inn in the 18th century but in young Lilian's time, Freddie Spear ran a taxi service from the site and also repaired cars. Once, when asked to take her to Cobbaton, Fred Spear drove Lilian all the way to Barnstaple instead, but she was too nervous to tell him until he got there!

Mr Coles had the bakery at Townsend, often called 'West End Bakery' over the years that followed. His name can still be seen on the wall of the house. Lilian can recall Mr Davey working at the bakery, he also ran a small shop there, selling 'all sorts; groceries, clothes, etc.' Lilian's mother once bought two dresses there for 7s.6d. each – 'a lot of money in them days'.

The last business Lilian can remember in 1935 was just past Townsend, roughly where Little Orchard is now. Another strange character called Mr Hobbs kept a cow there. He sold milk and also boots and shoes and did repairs, sometimes while you waited. Lilian and her future husband Dick obviously got on very well with this gentleman as he would give them 'luvly cream' and keep Dick talking

Above: Logging with Murch Bros. machines in the 1890s.

until 'gone midnight!'. He was also a local preacher and rather deaf, and would often start a sermon with 'Can't stay long, m'dears – got a cow goin' to calf...' all at the top of his voice. Apparently, more than once he was heard to say 'there's people in this congregation who owe me money, but us won't say who they are!' He was always greeting Lilian with 'yer 'er comes – dree foot an' 'alf a teddy!'

Lilian also says that in 1935, the station livestock market at Umberleigh was very active, especially on the second Tuesday of each month. The sale was mainly in cattle, along with sheep and a very large number of rabbits, which were all taken away to Exeter and London, on the train. Farmers would arrive early with their stock, then go over the bridge to the Rising Sun Hotel for 'breakfast'. At about 10 o'clock, Mr Gill the auctioneer would stand on the bridge and ring his great brass handbell for the farmers to emerge for the auction. After the sale, the animals gone, more 'breakfast' would be consumed!

In Umberleigh, Murch Bros. was well established by this time, and were well placed for the coming surge in agricultural mechanisation. A late-1930s advertisement describes them as 'makers of threshing machines, corn and manure drills, wheelwrights, machinists, implement agents and timber merchants'.

So the main pattern of trade in the community is thus mapped out and very little seemed to change until well after the war.

However, we move forward now to 1939 and our next contributor, Phyllis Lewis, can furnish us with more details and any changes that may have occurred. Phyllis moved to the village in 1924, when her father, Frank, started the bakery in East Street.

The bakery employed Percy Smoldon (whose son Alan was later to work as a butcher in the village), making white and brown bread, and 'double bakes' - the much loved crunchy biscuits - all baked in a wood and coke-fired Jones oven from Bristol.

One feature of life that Phyllis can recall was people bringing their Christmas dinner on a big iron tray, to cook in the bakery oven, presumably because their own were too small. They would walk with this splendid meal often from as far as New Buildings, that is, from right outside the village. Phyllis also remembers Mr and Mrs Webber who lived at the top of Hillhead. They had a small business making shoes for villagers.

Also at Hillhead, at Pippins, Bill Down had his horse and cart. He acted as haulier and general carrier. He had a thriving trade fetching and carrying all kinds of goods to Barnstaple and South Molton. Jim White also remembers that Bill was sometimes known to carry a hundredweight of coal up the hill on his own back, alongside the horse, so as to make it easier for the beast!

Pre-war economy is clearly shown here. At least two cobblers, two bakeries, tailors and several general stores - all demonstrating a community with a large degree of autonomy from the outside world where journeys to Barnstaple or South Molton, although occasionally undertaken, were quite unusual and often deemed unnecessary.

In addition to Lilian's memories, Phyllis can also remember that at Hillsview, George Boucher worked for a coal merchant Jack Gardiner, and next door there was a doctor's surgery. Phyllis remembers Doctors Seal, Mortimer and Nash.

Walking toward the Square, Rocklea, the former farmhouse on the right, housed Mr Rawle, a vet, while a little further along, the pub was still being run by Mr and Mrs Locke.

Miss Mules was still at Corner Cottage on the Square. As Phyllis recalls ''er was a funny ole stick, wadn' 'er!' Apparently, when weighing out sweets, if the weight wasn't exact, she would bite a sweet in half to make up the weight, then pop the remaining half back into the jar!

The house East Notts, as Phyllis remembers, was the home and workshop of Spencer Vivian, a ladies' and gents' tailor. An advertisement of the time declares 'riding breeches, a speciality' although Phyllis greatly admired a 'Vivian' suit. 'Wonderful suit – you'd never know but what it comed from a shop!'

Above: Petrol Station at Towns End.

Left to right: Bob Westacott, Philip Friendship, Jack Townsend, 1950s.

Right: Veterinary Rawle at Towns End outside Mr Hobbs the cobbler's, 1890s.

Spencer Vivian's other claim to fame was that he was a marvellous magician and children's entertainer. He was much in demand around the parish for his magic and puppet shows, both for private and public occasions.

Phyllis says when Mr and Mrs Gill moved from the shop (where Chittlechatter is now) to Townsend, Mr Gill had a hut near the garage, selling furniture,

china etc., and doing 'lots of buying and selling'. The garage, and Freddie Spear, were both still thriving it seems and the taxi service was still running people to South Molton. Fred often carried barbed wire in his taxi, at the same time as people. It was always a threat to ladies' stockings! Phyllis remembers the bakery opposite had passed, by 1939, to Harold Davey, who in turn employed George Rendell.

So we come to the Second World War. As with everywhere else, Chittlehampton parish was hugely affected. Men were called up (or volunteered), evacuees came into the community and the Government encouraged the mechanisation of the countryside. Clearly, a great leap forward was made in farm productivity, but the number of other small businesses in the parish seems to have been

maintained. Indeed, the decline in number of small shops and businesses that one might have expected following the war frankly did not happen until other influences (supermarkets and better transport) took a hand about twenty years later.

In 1945 after the war the story is provided by Ken and Nan Peters. Ken was born in the village in 1936 and between them Ken and Nan can remember several of the changes from the pattern of businesses established before the war.

In addition to the shops remembered by Lilian and Phyllis, Ken and Nan recall that Harry Potter was the blacksmith at Hillhead, presumably having taken over from Mr Vickery. Ken remembers him making gate hinges that 'are still with us now.'

The 'sweet-biting' Miss Mules was still on the corner of the Square, but Charlie Gard was the cobbler next door to her in the Square by this time. His advertisements boasted that 'Post Orders' were given 'Special Consideration'.

Mr Vivian was still tailoring and entertaining and Mr Burgess was still butchering, but Ken and Nan remember that Barley Mow Cottage was now a shop where Katie Short sold tea cakes, pop, tea, blocks of salt and paraffin. Much was the same at the Townsend part of the village, but Ken says that George Rendell had returned from the Navy. He worked once again in the bakery, this time for Fred Friendship, who seems to have taken it over from Mr Davey probably during the war years.

I am indebted to Ken and Nan's next door neighbour, Jim White. Jim was born at Brendon, on the northern edge of Exmoor in 1936 and moved into the village at the age of about two months. Jim was part of a large family that lived in the old Rolle Arms, and has so many wonderful memories of life in Chittlehampton that he has written them down in what amounts to his autobiography. Some of these memories he has kindly allowed me to use in our story of the years following the Second World War and the several changes that have taken place.

Above: *Ye Olde Shop, 1963.*

Above: *Mirabelle Gard outside the last shop in the Square, Footwear and Newsagents, 1960.*

Left: *Cobbles, the last tea room, 1998. Joan and Nigel Sinclair are outside.*

Below: *Howards Carpentry Shop at the end of the 19th century.*

Jim has several memories of the garage and taxi man, Freddie Spear. 'A proper village character - real eccentric, you!' As well as his taxi business, Freddie mended bicycles and cut people's hair. Jim can recall that one day Freddie was busy cutting someone's hair – in the bicycle repair shed, of course – when he suddenly remembered he was supposed to be meeting someone from the station with the taxi. It seems that not only did he drop tools and collect his passenger, but he went off on another job before he got back some hours later to find his 'victim' still waiting in the bicycle shed, afraid to go home with only half a haircut!

Murch Bros. have been the biggest family business in the parish for the last 120 years. The firm was founded in 1880 at Umberleigh by William Murch (blacksmith) and Thomas Murch (carpenter), and the original wooden building was situated on the same site as the present one.

In the early years the lathes were driven by water wheel and later by diesel engine (which also supplied power to some nearby homes) until electricity became available.

A big change at the western end of the village came when Harry and Lloyd Murch moved their business to Victoria House from Dorridge, near Umberleigh. In 1945, they built a large barn and opened a soon-to-be thriving agricultural contracting business, threshing corn, combing thatch, etc. They were joined soon afterwards by brother Bernard, on his return from the war.

Jim White can remember that steam engines used to pull the threshing machines as well as two reed combers. These were used to sort out the straight wheat straw for reed. At the back of the machine, when threshing out corn, there would be about six men tying the reed into bundles. They would use a piece of wire and a long hazel stick. These were called 'binds'. The bundles were called 'niches' and the men would take great pride in who could tie the tidiest niche. The reed was used to thatch local houses and ricks.

When working on local farms at harvest and threshing time, the men would go from farm to farm, staying the night along with their machines until the work was finished. Later in the 1950s, those steam engines, with their smoking chimneys and roaring engines, gradually went out of fashion and it was then that Harry and Lloyd bought diesel tractors – Field Marshalls, we're told. Now, although these machines had their own distinctive characters, they were certainly more efficient and there was probably less chance of setting light to your thatched roof as they went past! I'm told Bob Newton (who still lives in the village and knows a thing or two about tractors) kept one for years after they stopped being used for farm work 'and he could always start it, first time – on his own!'

This was a time of great expansion on the farms round about and the shops in the village certainly still seemed to be busy. The mechanisation of farming practice forced on farmers by the needs of the war, was followed by great demand for more food. Thus, wet pasture had to be drained as well as lots of other tasks relating to expansion. Harry and Lloyd Murch must have been especially busy at this time, threshing corn and reed combing.

Jim also remembers in the years after the war that Marian Waldon (later Marian Howard) would come up the hill from Deptford Farm with a pony and trap and a couple of small churns to deliver the milk to the village.

MEMORIES OF SHOPS AND BUSINESSES

Our next volunteer is Ruth Phillips (née Stone). Ruth was born in Barnstaple in 1943 and was brought up at Hillhead and attended the village school until 1953. She remembers watching the Coronation on the first television in Chittlehampton at the cottage at Hillhead, along with her family and many friends and neighbours.

Ruth went to school in South Molton until 1959, when she began work on her father's farm at Higher Biddacott, just to the north of the village. She married her husband Bob in 1964.

Ruth chose to take her 'walk through the village' in 1953, and she remembers many of the small businesses being unchanged since the war. However, she has a particularly good memory and recalls details vividly. For example, Harry Potter still had the forge. Ruth has fond memories of sitting in Harry's old rocking chair and watching him work. She remembers a large shiny nozzle from the old fire engine which was kept in the Square in former times. That fire engine was gone now, but the nozzle was still there, hanging on the wall in the forge. She also recalls a large notice outside the forge advertising the films to be seen at the South Molton Picture House.

There was a lady by the name of Dorothy Towell, who lived in Rose Cottage (next to where the old village stocks are now). She gave piano lessons which could be heard right down the road on a summer's day.

The pub was still there of course, run now by Jack Easton. The long-lasting Miss Mules, the cobbling Charlie Gard ('all repairs neatly executed'), the 'magic' Spencer Vivian, and Mr Burgess, who had his butchery at the rear of the present shop, were all still there. The building which is now Chittlechatter General Stores was at that time only one room up and down and was occupied by Mrs Garnett.

Ruth rode regularly through the village on her bicycle and remembers Townsend as a busy part of the community. Mr Gill still had his general dealing. Mrs Gill had the shop in what is now the Annexe and Freddie Spear, who lodged with the Gills, still had the taxi service and garage. Freddie's business seems to have been very busy because he ran four or five cars - most of them Austins - as Jim White recalls, 'and most of them forever breaking down!' – Jim says when he was a schoolboy, there was the famous occasion when the only way to get one of the cars home was for him to ride on the front wing, with the side bonnet up, carefully pouring petrol directly into the carburettor and trying not to spill a drop!

Charlie Leatherby lived in one of the cottages opposite the garage. Charlie had been a despatch rider during the war but Ruth remembers him as a busy and much-needed odd-job man, mason and chimney sweep. Charlie's wife, son Brian, granddaughter Pauline and two great-grand-daughters, Chloe and Leah, all live in the village today.

Ruth says the bakery on the corner at Townsend was run then by John Brace. He also sold groceries and general provisions. The business at Victoria House, run by Harry and Lloyd Murch, was very busy and was soon to expand.

Finally, as a young schoolgirl, Ruth remembers gathering apples from the farm orchard, and carrying them over the hill to Hancocks, the cider-makers at Clapworthy Mill, to be made into cider. She says many farmers' children did the same.

Right: *Froggy Street, 1890s.*

The next step in our journey is provided for us by Lorna Southcombe who is a real outsider to the village, coming as she does all the way from Umberleigh! Lorna was married in 1956 and moved to Chittlehampton in 1957. At first she lived at Townsend, but moved into Southview Bungalows in 1963, where she still lives with her son Lindsey. Lorna has chosen to take her walk for us in 1963, and the pattern, as described by Ruth, although similar, adds a few new names to the cast list.

At Hillhead, Mrs Baker was still selling paint and paper and pots and pans, but the forge seems to have gone cold. Around the corner, Jean Lewis was serving in the bakery shop, with Percy Smoldon and Bill Pratt doing the baking and going out on the delivery rounds.

Lorna remembers another house at that end of the village being used for a small business. This was Rocklea where Lorna says Reg Howard lived and ran a painting and decorating business from a workshop opposite. Reg also kept a small herd of cows which he milked in a shippen next to his house.

Right: *Wilf and young George Harris at Whey Farm with Wilf's first car – an Austin.*

Below: *Mr Pratt and Mr Smoldon delivering bread for Lewis the baker.*

MEMORIES OF SHOPS AND BUSINESSES

The Square was still a busy place for trade: the pub with Jack Easton behind the bar, Mr Gard, cobbler (boots, shoes, wellingtons and newspapers), Miss Mules (sweets, ribbons and hair slides), and Mr and Mrs Norman Smith at the Post Office.

Lorna remembers Mr and Mrs Short still running the shop in the Barley Mow, selling tobacco, and tinned foods, etc., but opposite in what is now the village stores, there was no shop yet. However, some years before, in 1952, Gordon and Kath Burgess had come to Greenfields (between the present stores and Townsend) and moved into a newly-built butcher's shop there. Lorna worked at the shop and made the pasties and hogs puddings every morning.

Although John Brace had the bakery when Lorna first arrived in the village, at the beginning of the 1960s, his cousin John Ford took over and ran a thriving business there for some years. He was later to run the garage at Umberleigh and lives there still, along with his wife, Edna. In fact, John and Edna's tenure of the West End bakery is a good example of a trend which is present in local businesses today, although was not really typical at the time. While the bakery shop supplied people in the parish, it also grew quickly and soon started selling outside the area. John tells me that at one point, the business had shops in South Molton and North Molton as well as five vans, delivering from Torrington to Simonsbath. So, while the number of enterprises certainly declined at this time, a few of the remaining ones began to serve a much larger market. The bakery was to close in the late '60s and the premises became an antiques shop for some years, run by Phil Mounter.

At Umberleigh, Lorna can remember Murch Bros. going strong, the Post Office at the Gables run by Mrs Dunn, and a cycle business next door run by her husband. Two ladies, Mrs Counter and Mrs Clark, ran the General Stores there.

We move forward now and come to the 1970s and the marvellous double act of Tracey Craze and Hazel Alford. Hazel (from a long-established local family) and daughter Tracey, have collaborated to produce their memories of the parish in 1975–76. Tracey was born in 1966 and attended school in Chittlehampton and in South Molton from 1971 until 1982. By 1975–76, when Tracey and Hazel are doing their

walk, we see a marked decline in the number of shops in the village. Clearly the much greater mobility of the population – even in a rural community – coupled with the rise of the supermarkets and DIY shops, made it much more difficult for village businesses to make a living.

Thus it was that the eastern end of the village was now much changed. The bakery had gone in the late 1950s to be replaced by a small antiques shop where Mr Keary lived and sold bric-a-brac, etc. He also played in a rock band – quite a change from times past!

Walking westwards, Tracey and Hazel remember that the next business was the public house – The Bell – in the Square. It was at this time that David and Susan Reed bought the pub from Whitbreads brewery. They still own it, though it's now mainly run by daughter Lynn and son-in-law Mark. In the Square, the Post Office was run by Mr Snow. He sold sweets and – says Tracey – Bay City Roller scarves.

Hazel recalls that the shop situated where Chittlechatter Stores is now was a Mace shop by this time, run by Mrs Gard and her daughter Hazel. They sold everything from paraffin to shoelaces and polish. Hazel remembers them delivering meat and vegetables around the area.

One of the main local businesses at that time was the butchery and greengrocery at Greenfields. Mr and Mrs Burgess had a thriving enterprise there, and were still supplying pasties and hogs puddings to the community. A certain young man was apprenticed there: Alan Smoldon, whose father had baked bread at the Lewis' bakery a generation before, was learning his trade. We hear more of Alan later.

Another delivery service was that of Bob Slape from Gambuston Farm, who Hazel remembers delivering fresh milk to the door and who continued to do so until 1989. Bob had delivered milk in the village for many years, and so had his father before him, in those days by tractor and link box. Apart from the contracting business which was still busy at Victoria House, Tracey and Hazel can remember the Howards selling eggs at Ash Farm. Bruce Bowden had his building business at Greenacres, and Ken Snow, a highly skilled wheelwright and carpenter at New Buildings, was just outside the village.

Colin and Audrey Bawden have kindly agreed to contribute their memories of the mid 1980s. Audrey has lived in Chittlehampton almost all her life and Colin moved here to work for John Ford at the bakery. They married in 1963.

The eastern end of the village had no shops at all, by now the first business Colin and Audrey can remember whilst walking through from east to west is that of Dennis Weaver. Dennis came to the village in 1984, he lives at Rocklea (formerly Pulhams) and runs a busy school of motoring from the premises.

In the Square there were two enterprises: The Bell Inn was still busy and next door but one from it the Post Office and shop was in the hands of Pauline and Paddy Steer. Later to take over the village general stores, Pauline and Paddy, along with their son Ian, dispensed newspapers, stamps and much good cheer to all and sundry.

Walking up the street, Colin and Audrey remember a charming flower shop next to the present Chittlechatter General Stores. Jenny Alford had started up a year or so before, selling sprays of flowers, small posies, Christmas wreaths and all things floral. After a few years, she moved the flower shop to Umberleigh and, along with her husband Barry, combined it with a much needed general stores.

Back in Chittlehampton, next door to the flower shop, Colin and Audrey recall Alan and Jenny Smoldon taking over the shop premises in 1984. After considerable renovations, the shop was relaunched with Jenny 'front of house' and Alan, by now an expert butcher following his apprenticeship with Gordon Burgess, in charge of the butchery. Alan also operated what seems to have been a huge daily delivery round in the area. Every afternoon he took in Chittlehamholt, Bradbury, Bray Mill, Warkleigh, Satterleigh and Umberleigh, delivering everything possible to outlying farms and settlements.

Colin and Audrey remember no shops or small businesses at Townsend at this time, the garage and then the bakery having ceased trading some years before. However, at Victoria House, Barry Murch had taken over from his father Harry some years previously, and was busy on the digger contracting side. No more threshing now, the age of the combine-harvester was well and truly with us.

Roger Cockram outside his pottery.

© Cobbaton Photographic

© Cobbaton Photographic

Top: *Mary Parker, Gloria Fricker, Sandra Steele, Sonia Lishman and Pauline Heale outside Chittlechatter Stores.*

Left: *The Bell*

Below: *Umberleigh village shop during the 1970s.*

MEMORIES OF SHOPS AND BUSINESSES

So we come to our present decade. I have chosen to round off the survey myself. I arrived in the village in 1986 from Ashreigney. My immediate family comes from Barnstaple, but I trace my ancestors back to Swimbridge in 1750.

Having bought Victoria House and buildings from Barry Murch in 1986, I started on the long job of converting the barns and setting up my pottery studio and shop. I was very pleased to find a site with existing planning permission on the edge of such a lovely village. We now have a studio/workshop and kiln room along with an adjoining showroom/shop in the barns which once held harvesters and grain stores.

My walk through the village is different from the one Lilian took. It is eighteen months now since she and Lorna sat with me, my daughter Lucy and a full teapot in her kitchen, to remember how things were in 1935.

Lisa Scattergood and Simon Heath live just outside the village, on the road to Filleigh. They really are recent arrivals, having moved here in March 1999. Their business is design. Lisa is a calligrapher and lettering artist and Simon is a graphic designer and arts worker. Together, they trade under the name of xHeight Design and are already actively contributing to the life of the community – not least in their design of this volume.

At the eastern end of the village itself there are no forges, bakeries or general stores, but the post-war changes in business activity in the parish are clearly shown by the example of Shaun Mansfield. He and his wife Keri bought the forge and adjoining house in 1995, from where Shaun runs a telecom and data networks business called Mansfield Telecom. He sells and installs this equipment not only in the village, but throughout Devon and, indeed, nationwide.

Below: Pat and Sian Murch at The Tack Store.

THE BOOK OF CHITTLEHAMPTON

Dennis Weaver is still running the motoring school from his home at Rocklea. Andrew Murch and his family live opposite Dennis, or thereabouts. Andrew runs a building business from the property, building and repairing houses all over the area.

My walk takes me past (and sometimes into) the Bell Inn. Still owned by David and Susan Reed and run by their daughter Lynn and son-in-law Mark, it seems to be the perfect village pub. The Bell attracts people from far outside the parish for all sorts of events, from live music and quiz nights to Harvest Festival services and auctions. It is always guaranteed to afford the visitor, stranger or regular, a warm welcome and an excellent pint. It is also the main focus for most of the village sports, as well as acting as the most efficient method so far invented of spreading local news! I love it.

For a couple of years, until this summer, Nigel and Joan Sinclair ran a tea-room in the Square, in the former Post Office, now Telegraph Cottage, and splendidly converted to a private dwelling. Incidentally, the single telegraph pole in the pub's back garden was the first in the village bringing the 'telegraph' to the Post Office in the Square. As someone said, 'Not a lot of people know that'.

Today, walking westwards from the Square, the first business we come to is run from the Westcotts' home at New House. Mr Westcott and his sons have run a thriving thatching business for at least twenty years throughout the village and throughout North Devon. Their work has been an essential feature of village life, and with so many thatched houses in the area it continues to be very much in demand.

Next is the village shop, now called Chittlechatter. Owned by Pauline Steer, the shop is run today by Sonia and Derek Lishman, and having changed hands a few times in recent years, it now looks set for a period of stability under the present enthusiastic management.

Moving on with my walk, Barley Mow is now a private house, as is Greenfields. Incidentally, Gordon Burgess can still be seen in the village most days, delivering pasties and hogs puddings for sale in the shop, though he and his wife have lived in South Molton for several years now.

Opposite the village hall Ian Rogers lives with his family. Ian is a skilled plumber and operates his business both locally and more widely in North Devon.

At Danmar (roughly where Mr Gill had his bric-a-brac hut and garage many years ago) John Palmer runs his joinery and construction business with his son. John has recently gone into partnership with another builder, so Palmer Birch now have a team of six, allowing them to take on a wider range of work.

We have two thatchers in the village. The more recent is John Jones who takes on work within a twenty-mile radius of his home in Mayflower Close.

At Townsend in 1997, Richard Tully and his family moved into the old bakery house and building. Richard runs a business making special fabric products which sell all over the world.

Barry Murch and family did not move far from Victoria House in 1986. They built a bungalow two doors away at Hobbs Lea (remember Mr Hobbs?), from where Barry runs his digger/contracting business.

At the pottery we are busier than ever. Work is divided into several categories. The useful or domestic pottery I design with Giles who works for me, and my wife Ros helps us both to decorate it. My individual/art pieces are based on drawings I make of water and its natural surroundings (ponds and marine pools, etc.), so that fish and frogs usually figure quite strongly! Ros makes a small range of ceramic figures and candlesticks, and also exhibits her beautiful paintings (and prints) in the showroom and elsewhere in the country.

The third builder in our parish is David Roe. David lives at Little Winson and runs his busy company from home.

Just across the road is Winson Farm. It's the home of Robert and Ann Page, and houses Ann's hairdressing business.

Still in the parish, Tim Hickman and his family moved into Whey Farm in 1998. Tim makes picture frames, trading under the name The Watergate Picture Framing Co.

2,000,000
HARRIS'S Late Flatpole Cabbage Plants.

The above is the result of several years' careful selection, and raised from my own Prize Winning Stock, and cannot fail to give satisfaction to all buyers.

BICYCLES of all the leading makes, both new and second hand, on hire and purchase.

J. HARRIS, JUN., SEEDSMAN, &c., CHITTLEHAMPTON.

THE NEW BAKERY AND GROCERY STORES,
TOWNSEND, CHITTLEHAMPTON.

J. COLE

Begs to thank his customers for past support, and to inform them, that he has a large stock, which he offers at lowest prices, and is open to compete with any of the surrounding Towns.

Try our Special Blend Tea, 5½d. per ¼ lb., or 3 lbs. for 5/-

☞ ORDERS PROMPTLY ATTENDED TO.

Agent for any kind of China or Earthenware.

G. MULES,
FAMILY TAILOR, BREECHES MAKER,
WOOLLEN DRAPER, HATTER & OUTFITTER,
The SQUARE, CHITTLEHAMPTON.

A large and varied assortment of Patterns to select from.

Mourning Orders promptly Executed.   Mackintoshes to Order.

J. HOWARD

Begs to thank his numerous customers and friends for their kind patronage and support in the past, and now begs to call their attention to the increased facilities he has to execute all kinds of orders for Carpenters' and Joiners' Work, Cottage and Kitchen Furniture of modern design, and strongly made, also Wheelwrights' Work of every description, all of the best materials and workmanship and at reasonable prices. ☞ ESTIMATES AND DESIGNS ON APPLICATION.

Sittings of Eggs from Prize-winning Plymouth Rocks and Minorcas are now ready for early hatching : also from the Special Cross (for laying) Minorca-Leghorn which produce profitable Autumn and winter Layers. Special Rat-proof Chicken Coops with movable Floors and Food protectors at reasonable prices : also portable Hen Houses ; prices and designs for which can be had on application.

 Insure your Goods and Property in the Sun Fire Office } Established 180 Years.
Insure your Life, at lowest rates in the Sun Life Office }

AGENT :--J. HOWARD, CHITTLEHAMPTON.

At Brightley, across the valley from Tim, newcomer David Battle is a furniture maker and restorer who has recently moved from London with his wife and family to set up his workshop in our parish.

Sian Murch has opened a new equestrian business at the Murch Bros. site, selling everything from tack and saddlery to feed stuffs. Sian's husband Pat has launched an antiques emporium which he runs with his son Rob in the same building. Dan and Anto still serve the community's engineering needs there as well as, ensuring the continuity of the Murch family business.

Also by the bridge at Umberleigh is the Gables Tea Rooms and Guest House. The Gables is owned and run by Tony and Myra Pring. They purchased the business in 1990 from Mr and Mrs Riccard, and are busy all year round providing accommodation for a wide range of clients. In the summer, they welcome many travellers with delicious ice cream or a cup of tea. Tony also runs a business as a plumber and electrician. It seems there are very few skills not represented in the parish.

There has been a Post Office in Umberleigh for fifty one years. Judy Leach learnt her skills there at the age of fifteen, but only took over the enterprise last year. The previous postmistress was Mrs Rishton who ran the office for twenty years. Many's the time I have driven furiously down the hill to buy a stamp from her and catch the last post of the day which is just that bit later than the collection from Chittlehampton.

When Lilian remembered 1935, she came up with fifteen shops and small businesses in Chittlehampton. This dropped to about seven shops and businesses in 1975. If we count all the self-employed and small enterprises in the parish today, we have a marked increase in numbers and can see the emergence of a thriving, varied community of craftsmen and traders. I see no reason why this should not continue.

The other working backbone of this parish is of course farming. It is not in our brief here, but naturally remains, in spite of very hard times at the moment, the core working activity in the area.

Below: *Council road workers, 1930s.*

Transportation and the Railway

by Rae Knight, Frank Kidwell and Cliff Gregory

Transport has always been important to the growth and maintenance of village life. Long ago, livestock and produce had to be carried to the nearest market town, and as the village thrived, more and swifter methods had to be found to keep up with supply and demand.

Later, some charming and attractive methods of delivery were established; Taffy Cole and friend (in what look suspiciously like demob suits with a hint of Chicago 1930, *below*) seem to have had a very stress-free method of bringing goods to the village.

Farms have always had a variety of carts and wagons to be put to use as floats for the fête, carriages for the pageant and even taxis for weddings and other functions. In the 1920s and '30s the charabanc was a very popular vehicle (*below*). A kind of forerunner of the current people carrier, it could convey most of the community on picnics and trips to the beach.

The horse was, and still is, a very important part of the community. Until around the 1950s, the blacksmith's shop was a kind of drop-in centre of communication and gossip.

The coming of the railway changed much of rural life. Towns and other villages became accessible; luggage, freight, people and animals could be collected and delivered so much more quickly than via the patient effort of the plodding horse. Umberleigh Railway Station was on the Southern Railway line. Little is known about its very early working days, but one touching reference is worth recounting. Harry Lethbridge had fought in the First World War at the terrible battle of Ypres where he was wounded, and taken prisoner. In October 1915, one year after his capture, Harry stepped off the train from London at Umberleigh Station to be met by pony and trap, and was transported as far as Deptford Hill, where a party of schoolboys unhitched the pony and dragged the trap in true triumphal style to his parents' front door.

The station worked on, reliably and safely carrying out its duties through the post-war period and the Depression, and right through another world war. Then, on the last day of 1949, Frank Kidwell came to Umberleigh to serve as the station's Leading Porter Signalman. 'A grade' says Frank, 'which allowed my railway employers to expect me to do any job, of any sort, at any time!' He moved with his young bride into one of the Railway Cottages. 'She being a city girl' says Frank, 'didn't know that places existed that used pump water, paraffin lamps, primus cooking, a boiling copper for washing and, the *piece de resistance*, the 'sentry box' with a bucket in the garden!' It was the start, Frank remembers, of such wonderful years living in a community. 'Two houses, one front path, one porch with two front doors should be a recipe for friction, but having super neighbours with six kids was educational, and we loved it.'

Frank worked hard. 'The signalling duty was the more responsible', he says, 'because whereas the other duties were related to money or goods, this involved passengers' lives and we were made very aware of this and not allowed to go solo in the [signal] box until certificated to do so.' Frank's description of the safety measures taken in those days to avoid collision is well worth noting, and adds greatly to the feeling of comfort and security those now-disused methods must have conveyed.

Above: *Bill Passmore handing the tablet.*

Below: *Frank Kidwell at the Ilfracombe signal box in 1962.*

© Clifford Gregory

'This was the hey-day of the steam train. The Devon Belle and the Atlantic Coast Express were names to conjure with... For them to go onto the single track, of which Umberleigh was the start, a token had to be obtained from a machine with the co-operation and co-ordination of the signalman at Portsmouth Arms [Station]. This ensured once a token (or tablet, as it was known) was obtained at one end of the section, no other train could enter that section. It was quite a thrill to stand at the platform edge and pass or take a tablet from a racing, steaming noisy engine, with the fireman hanging out of the cab, arm outstretched. This was fine in daylight but somewhat challenging in the dark with rain pelting down.

'I remember one afternoon, the train had overrun the platform and only one lady passenger wanted to alight... so I suggested she lower herself to me, but she jumped out, almost flattening me... One of the most unusual duties was to go into the auction field and collect livestock from the pens and move them into the railway pens, ready for loading into cattle wagons. My job was to make sure the wagons were clean, correctly labelled for their destination and the floor covered in sawdust. Sheep and cattle didn't pose any problems, but pigs were a law unto themselves! It was a condition laid down that sows and boars were to be separated. That condition was obviously composed by a morally pious city person who had never been in a pen with six sows and a boar in a separate one! A frustrated boar with tusks firmly implanted under the partition would suddenly and effortlessly cast the barrier between himself and the lights of his eye into the air... ! Broom heads were often broken on a charging head, and there were occasions when a pig would slip onto the track between the wagon side and the loading dock wall. Seven stone of panicked pig takes some stopping!

As well as clean and prepare the wagons, load recalcitrant stock, operate the signals and keep the platforms and cloakrooms tidy, Frank was often asked to fill in cheques for farmers who were a little uncertain how to do so. 'Being one of the trusted community was a wonderful part of small station life' he says. 'The parcels to be distributed were sorted out, and the reputable Mr Fred Spear was called in with his taxi. He knew everything and everyone within a ten-mile radius. Chickens, a calf, Great Universal parcels – you name it – Fred carried it. A wonderful chap from Townsend.

'A very special occasion was the day of the Lynmouth flood – 1953 that was, and for us, it started with the postman coming across from South Molton. He came over a hump-back bridge at around four-thirty in the morning and the van went under water. A quick retreat had to be made, but gradually the water rose and came up over the bank,

© Clifford Gregory

© Clifford Gregory

Top: *West Country or Battle of Britain steam train heading for Exeter through the snow in January, 1963.*

Above: *141 Squadron.*

Below: *Showing auction pens and pump house beyond the goods shed. West Country/Battle of Britain going up the line.*

Bottom: *Through the floods of 1978.*

© Clifford Gregory

© Beaford Photographic Archive

near the bridge, close to Mr Dunn's cycle shop and flowed on towards the auction field.

Eventually it cut off the station approach road and filled to the doorstep of Railway Cottages. As each train arrived, Bill Passmore and I ferried the passengers across the flooded road on the station barrow. Bark off-cuts from the sawmill floated downstream and the railway bridge supports became dangerously clogged with timber and debris. Gradually it receded and I spent days of spare time getting timber out of the river and cutting it up. No chain-saw then. It was bow saw and hard work...

'Haymaking and corn harvesting would be attended voluntarily and work would go on until dark without reward. Later in the year though, a bag of swedes, a rabbit, a lump of salmon, all sorts, would appear on the doorstep overnight. In the midst of an evening's gardening a voice would shout through the hedge, 'Come on, I've had enough for a while' and everything stopped whilst a crowd of us made our way to the pub for a quickie.

'The railway was the local lifeline for so many. Children were regulars, going into Barnstaple for senior education, and the eight-forty morning train had daily and weekly users. Market day had the pannier hampers and baskets going in and the five-twenty-four afternoon train from Town Station brought home wives, children, calves and very often husbands who found some difficulty in keeping the platform steady!' And talking of Town Station! 'As I said', recalls Frank, 'Umberleigh was on the Southern Railway line – so that's the SR. We also had the Great Western Railway coming into Barnstaple – so that's GWR. Those who worked for them used to say GWR stood for 'God's Wonderful Railway', but we called it something different. We called it the 'Go When Ready line!'

Not every job was blessed with success and grateful thanks however. Frank recalls an attempt to provide that little extra service that marked so much of his years' work at the station. 'I got my bicycle out to deliver a box of day-old chicks. Instead of appreciation, there was admonishment' he says sadly. 'I didn't pronounce the lady's name right so my delivery service was not appreciated. Forelock touched, and 'Yes Ma-am. Sorry Ma-am.' But they were mostly good times. Summertime provided the opportunity to go to the pool at the lower side of the railway bridge for a cooling swim. On one occasion a very quick exit was made when we were joined by a three foot grass snake! I could go on, but changes come and I got promotion in 1953 to Mortehoe and Woolacombe and, after eight years, on again to Ilfracombe from 1960 to 1966.

'Happy days and good friends at Umberleigh where the living was so kind to us. We left with heavy hearts and great affection for so many.'

About ten years later Owen Gregory was appointed Station Master at Umberleigh. This post included the control of Portsmouth Arms where Bill Butt was signalman, and Chapleton where Wilf Osman served. Owen's son Cliff remembers his first visit to the signalbox at Umberleigh: 'It had the familiar look and smell of all signal boxes: polished brass and wood, together with the smell of oil, methylated spirits and coke fires. The brown lino surrounding the lever frame was highly polished to the point of squeaking underfoot. The usual slightly oiled duster hung over one of the levers ready for the next summons by bell code from either of the adjacent signal boxes. These rags were used to protect the handles from going rusty from the grip of sweating hands. A heavy kettle was on the stove which was permanently lit in all signal boxes. The train register was open, ready for the next entry with an old nibbed pen sitting in its inkwell. Above the lever frame was a row of highly polished brass domed bells and their instrument cases, each labelled Up Advance or Down Advance with a semi-circular brass label. Just inside the door stood the upright red token instrument with the token ready for release to the next train through.'

The exchange of tablets or tokens with the driver of a moving train was always fascinating to those who remember seeing it done. As Cliff Gregory says, 'It was a manoeuvre which looked easy enough, but a slip on the part of either signalman or driver could result in many minutes lost, as a normally non-stop train would have to be brought to a standstill for the tokens to be recovered. The procedure of issuing tablets or tokens was not generally understood, but the theory was simple: where a railway line is single track, in order to avoid a head-on collision with a train from the opposite direction a token must be carried by the driver. It can only be released from its housing or instrument by the signalman in the box in advance because he will have placed the one carried by the driver of the previous train into its housing, guaranteeing that the line was now clear of traffic.'

Left: *Edmund Davies.*

How different it is now! 'After Beeching,' says Cliff, 'railways everywhere went into decline. The line from Barnstaple through to Eggesford was made into a single track. This meant that staff were no longer needed to man a signal box at Umberleigh. The Booking Office was closed and the station became an unstaffed halt. Sad days. All freight traffic to Umberleigh came to an end and agricultural machinery for Murch Bros. was transported by road... My mother continued to tend the gardens on the platform, but the competition for Best Kept Station in which Umberleigh had done so well for many years became a thing of the past... '

Right: *John Lake, Owen Gregory, Roy Samson and Jock McMath outside Umberleigh signal box, 1966.*

Below: *Night-time 63 class, 1970s.*

Pictures Of Village Life

Looking Back

Mrs Gill

Mrs Rawle

1927 School Concert Party

The wedding of Alfred and Bessie Upton in 1913.

Village Weddings

Sid and Gert Mayne-Bater

Harry and Ida Murch

Bob and Ruth Phillips

Village Weddings

Jimmy and Ruth Heathcote

Bill and Lorraine Castle

Kevin and Nicola Hussell

Above: *School egg-rolling contest, 1998.*

Left: *Behind: Pearl Gard; front from left to right: Hazel Dallyn, Nigel Gard, Margaret Cook, 1968.*

Facing page: *Headmaster Richard Hore and children, c.1900.*

Schools In The Parish

Chittlehampton Church of England Primary School

by Carole Henderson-Begg

There has been a school in Chittlehampton since 1865. Records show that:

By deed of 20 December 1865, the Right Hon. Hugh Earl Fortescue, the Hon. Mark George Kerr Rolle, and sixteen others, being the trustees of certain lands in the parish of Chittlehampton held for ecclesiastical purposes, under the authority of the Schools Sites Act, freely and voluntarily and without any valuable consideration granted to the vicar and church wardens of the parish of Chittlehampton and their successors for ever a piece of ground formerly the site of certain poor houses situate on the west side of the tower of the church of Chittlehampton and containing in length 152 feet or thereabouts and in breadth 50 feet or thereabouts... to hold unto and to the use of the said vicar and church wardens for the time being of the same parish for the purposes of the said Act and to be applied as a site for a school for poor persons of and in the said parish and for the residence of the teacher or teachers of the said school and for no other purpose, such school to be under the management and control of the vicar for the time being of the parish and the said church wardens for the time being thereof, and of the said Hugh Earl Fortescue and the Hon. Mark George Kerr Rolle, their heirs and assigns so long as they should be bona fide members of the Church.

It was built as a mixed Public Elementary School for 200 children and when William Bulled was schoolmaster the school is recorded as having been endowed with £10.4s. annually by Lord Rolle. The New Council School at Umberleigh, for eighty six children, was not built until 1913.

Above: *Headmaster Bevan with pupils, c.1910.*

However, the Revd John Andrews records in his book of Chittlehampton that fifty years before this school was opened ' ...a school, the Master of which was paid £6 a year, held on Sundays and Saints' Days, was established in 1815'. The rules can with fair confidence be ascribed to Charles Chichester (the then incumbent). It was to be conducted on Dr Bell's system, by which the children largely taught each other. Books used were to be solely those published by SPCK (Society for the Propagation of Christian Knowledge), writing and arithmetic were not to be taught. The children were to ' ...meet at 8am and, with intervals for divine service were to continue until 7.30p.m., or in winter until dusk.' Here the religious ends of the institution were paramount, and children constantly reminded of the sins of pride, pilfering, idleness, swearing, lying, disobedience, etc.; the aim of the school apparently being to 'check and reform vicious habits and all tendencies towards them in the rising generation'.

The earliest school logbook available dates from 1 June 1863, when a new code came into operation. Most of the early comments refer to attendance, inattentiveness, lessons badly learnt or much improved and punishments. The punishments were for disobedience or idleness, for losing their place in reading, for failing to learn their lessons, for coming too late or for playing marbles after 9a.m. It also refers to pupils who left to go to London, Birmingham and in one case Australia. Other entries include: '17th July 1867 – Maria Sey put to grief (for eating apples), Mary Watts kept in five minutes for making a mistake (29 September 1869), and 'The classroom fire lighted today for the first time (24 November 1869).'

The first recorded schoolmaster was John Pedler, a certified teacher who worked until 28 April 1876. On his retirement ' ...he was presented with a purse of twenty sovereigns as a token of his faithful service during the period of thirty five years' which means he became head in 1841!

The previous report stated 'this school is doing uncommonly well. The weak point is the reading, which is hardly loud enough in the lower classes, and is wanting in expression in the upper ones.' There is also a reference to a night school at this time.

Later reports were very variable. In June 1874 a report stated that 'This school has on the whole passed a very fair examination. Singing is very fair. Needlework is improving. Mr Pedler is an

industrious and painstaking teacher.' But when William Denley became head certified teacher on 2 January 1882 he found 'that the work throughout the school was in a very backward state'. In the 1860s pupils took days off for tilling potatoes, or picking stones or blackberries.

At the beginning of the century there were 180 children on the roll and the schoolmaster was Richard Hore. The amount of the grant received was £34.5s., of which £20 was the Headmaster's salary. The Revd J H B Andrews recounts that back in 1892 school dinners cost 1d. or 4d. for five, and that over sixty children took them. On Monday and Wednesday there was pea soup and bread, on Tuesday and Thursday it was bread and corned beef sandwiches and tea, and on Friday bread and jam, and bread and butter with cocoa. These were organised by the archdeacon's wife. Sadly he records that 'Even at 1d. a working man with a large family could not afford them and they ceased in 1896.'

The closure of Cobbaton School in 1912, and much later of Warkleigh and Chittlehamholt in 1948, brought children in from north and south, and the opening of Umberleigh School in 1913 took children away from the western side of the parish. In August 1905 'Charlie Lewis was awarded a scholarship of £30 per annum, tenable for two years, at the Devon County School' – one of thirteen selected from over 400 candidates.

In 1907, when the school broke up for Christmas holidays, the occasion was marked by an entertainment given by the scholars. The programme included recitations: 'A Stitch in Time' by Gladys Murch and Winnie Whitehorn, 'I Wonder Why' by Willie Ford, 'Bunnies' by Lionel Howard, 'Keeping School' by M Waldron, K Hall, S Watts, H Howard, C Holland, A Lethbridge, J Tucker, F Trim and J Huxtable, and songs: 'The Doll's Quarrel' by G Taylor, E Goss and A Down, 'Holy Night' by M Waldron, K Breayley, E Cocks, K Hall, G Pennington, C Chapple, J Tucker and A Lethbridge, 'The Burial of Sir John Moore' by F Trim and 'Nigger Dialogue' by W Watts, H Spear, W Gaydon, H Gaydon and E Lock, and also class songs.

In 1908 there were 142 children on the roll, the movable screen was in place and the logbook entry for 26 October records that:

There are some girls in the senior class who passed an excellent examination showing a very full knowledge of both Prayer Book and Bible subjects. The boys did not do so well.

In July 1909 Katherine Hall, Gladys Taylor and Phyllis Taylor won national prizes for needlework. Five others got a Certificate of Honour and seven a 'Memorable Mention'. This gratifying result was commemorated by closing the school at 3.35p.m., successful scholars being given a healthy clap, a success which was repeated the following year reflecting great credit on Miss E Dinnicombe.

In those days the school was closed for periods of several weeks by outbreaks of scarlet fever or whooping cough. Other one-day closures were for the rooms to be used for Harvest Tea, for a polling station, or for a Club Dinner and Dance in connection with the Friendly Society. On 17 September 1909 it was closed for Barnstaple Pleasure Fair, while on 29 June 1917 the school was closed 'for a fortnight in order that the older children may assist in the hay harvest'.

In the years between the First and Second World Wars a warning bell was rung at 8.55a.m. and again at 9a.m. when all children had to be in their class lines ready to go in to Assembly which consisted of a prayer, a hymn and a scripture reading before the start of lessons.

Children from Stowford, Cobbaton and outlying farms had to walk to school. Wet clothes were hung on the high fireguard around the tortoise stove in each classroom. Children who couldn't go home to lunch brought sandwiches and a hot drink was made for them.

Health checks were regular. A dentist came and also a doctor. A teacher kept height and weight records and checked hair for nits. Other visitors included a scripture Inspector – a Mr Hawkins is remembered as one who gave the children tests on the Bible, and Mr Westcott was one of the Attendance Officers. He used to travel around in a pony and trap. The Reverend Mortimer's wife held sewing classes at the Vicarage for school and church funds.

Each year Empire Day was celebrated on 24 May. The Union Jack was flown outside and May Lethbridge, Nance Tudball and Doris Jones remember Mr and Mrs Thorold coming down from Hudscott to give them a bun and an orange after watching the children dance round the maypole and sing, the songs being taken from *British Songs for British Boys and Girls* and then, to their delight, they had the rest of the day off. The practices for maypole dancing were held in the dinner hour in the field where Barnstaple Close was later built and Mrs Lean would take her gramophone and records.

Ascension Day was a holiday. Harvest Tea was held in school as well as the Sunday School Christmas treat to which children from Umberleigh were invited. Parents arrived after tea for a social when the children received their Sunday School prizes.

Sports Day was held at the end of the summer term, and throughout the year Abbots Hill was used for football and netball. While Mr Baskin was Headmaster he formed '...a lovely Mandolin Band which played at concerts and sometimes for the school hymns.' May Lethbridge was a member of this band.

In those days hunt balls were held in the school room when long dresses were worn. These occasions were 'quite a do!' Then there was the annual Club Walk organised by the Friendly Society. The children and villagers marched up to the Vicarage behind Torrington Town Band where they danced a furry dance in front of the Carnival Queen and her attendants. Doris Jones remembers that Winnie Dean, Hilda Clark and Alvina Murch played these roles one year. This event also included maypole dancing, country dancing, a fancy-dress competition for children and various stalls as well as the main attraction – the teas!

In 1936 the University College of the South West directed a pageant drama which was connected with a pilgrimage organised by the Church Union, the first since the reformation, to raise funds to put the tower in a proper state of repair. Sadie Kelly played the part of Saint Hieritha. She was the model for Saint Hieritha's statue on the church tower. The last pageant depicting the pilgrimage was in 1974 and included a march from the village hall to the Square where the story of St Hieritha was enacted by villagers and schoolchildren. The part of St Hieritha was played by Stephanie Thome, and the children performed a rain dance which seemed to have the desired effect each time it was rehearsed! At the time of writing the village is preparing another performance of the pageant for the millennium year. It is an event to look forward to, continuing as it does the history and traditions of this parish.

During the Second World War 'Toc H', where Hope Cottage is now, was used as a kitchen and canteen to feed village children and evacuees who were attending school. On 31 May 1940 notice was received that 'Everard Howard has passed the Scholarship Examination for Barnstaple Boys' Grammar School,' On 13 June 1940 evacuees, plus teachers and helpers, arrived about 6p.m. and billets were found. The following day the evacuees were assembled in the Square, they went for a walk because seating accommodation made formal schooling impossible.

Facing Page: *Chittlehampton School, 1956.*
Left to right, back row: Malcolm Peters, Colin White;
front row: Peter Down, David Peters, Dicko White, John Buckingham, Chris Webber, [   ], Gordon Rice.

The school closed as usual during August that year, but remained open for any children who wanted to attend. Teachers took holidays in rotation. The annual inspection for that year reported that:

...the evacuated children and the Devon children are settling down very well indeed and all the teachers are doing their best to ensure a good working arrangement. The organisation of the school is on a sound basis and the results which have already been achieved are worthy of commendation.

In January 1947 the school became the Junior Mixed School, so seniors were transferred to South Molton Modern. Then in March 1952 a special meeting of Managers under Prebendary Griffin agreed to apply for Aided Status. The LEA suggested that it would be better to build a new three-class school for ninety children rather than adapt the existing limited premises. However, by 1959 sites which could have served for the school had been used for housing, so the new school would have had to have been built at some distance from the church, making it more difficult for church and school to work together.

In 1956 Dick Baylis was appointed Headmaster and in August, together with his wife Wynne, and three children, Elizabeth, David and Jane, moved into

School House which had been bought by Mrs Andrews, the vicar's wife, for use by the current headmaster.

The bell still rang every morning to call children to school. Evelyn Beer (née Westcott) recalls never leaving home 'until we heard that bell ring.' The job of ringing the bell was one that older children liked – so some must have got to school early!

The school day varied depending on which class you were in. Infant lessons included counting with little shells, story time and writing in a daily diary about what had been done the previous evening. Lessons for the middle class included scripture, maths, more detailed diary writing, games and PE. In the top class there was a much broader education including catechism on Wednesday mornings with the vicar, and nature walks around the village. The children had four books – English, maths, a diary and a jotter. The desks had ink wells filled by the caretaker or the head boy and the pens were a nib on the end of a stick.

The school day finished at 4p.m. with afternoon prayers said as everyone stood behind their tidied desks, and then staff took turns on bus duty, waiting with the children and seeing them on to the two buses when they arrived.

The school playground was the Square, and teacher Mrs Benn and pupil John Symons remember the invisible line from Gard's shop (Cobble Cottage) to the village pump and up to the lych gate. That was the boundary which no-one dared to cross. The playground games were the usual ones – skipping, conkers in season, racing marbles, etc. Everyone had a third pint bottle of milk at break time and lunch was served in the village hall as it is to this day.

The present pottery shed at the top of the steps behind the school was then the school toilets. There was water there but the tank had to be filled by a hosepipe attached to a tap in the school. It was one of Mr Baylis' first jobs in the morning to lift one of the older boys up to check that the tank was full. There was no electricity so for evening events torches were made available.

The school was heated by 'tortoise' stoves which Mrs Headon, the school caretaker, used to light before the morning session began. Mrs Benn recalls one occasion when a pipe from the stove in her classroom got blocked and Rosemary Cole suddenly collapsed on to the floor. The supply teacher was called to assist and the whole school had to be evacuated to the church to avoid carbon-monoxide poisoning.

The school was still used for social and fund-raising events, as well as village meetings.

There was the annual Missionary Sale and another for the Mothers' Union.

SCHOOLS IN THE PARISH

The school held a jumble sale each year to raise money for the Christmas party. Wynne Baylis says 'I will always remember Mrs Parkhouse arriving with a tin bath full of home-grown Brussel sprouts which were sold very quickly.' Mothers were asked to make cakes for the party and Dick Baylis offered that his mother would make a ginger cake – she had never made one in her life!

Also at Christmas there was a carol service and a Nativity play. The children expected leading parts as they moved up the school. There was no set script which allowed for some variations such as:

Joseph: You'll have to let me in. My
              wife's having a baby.

Innkeeper: Well, it's nothing to do with me!

Facing page top: *Children in the Square in the 1920s.*

Facing page bottom: *Maypole dancing in 1936.*

Below: *School trip to Bristol Zoo in 1971 with Headmaster Mr Baylis.*

There were a few school trips to Bristol Zoo, the canal ride from Tiverton to Sampford Peverell, and of course the Sunday-School outing to Exmouth or a similar beach when each child was given money for ice creams.

The School Camp at Loxhore was an annual adventure. Children were taken under canvas for a week. Time was spent walking on the moor, visiting Pinkery Pond and walking from Watersmeet to Lynmouth. There was always a day for parents to visit and join in the fun.

In 1978 Jean Benn retired at the end of the summer term and Mr Baylis the following Christmas. Ian Henderson-Begg was to be the next Headmaster with Mrs Coe the new Deputy Head. The Henderson-Begg family moved into the village in deep snow on 2 January 1979, and all four sons attended the school.

Above: *Mrs Benn and her class of 1972.*
Left to right, back row: Alan Sheath, Sarah Strudwick, Winston Thorn, Sallie Slape, David White, Simon Nutt, Monica Needs, Christopher Thorn, Roland Davis, Monica Phillips;
front row: Gary Phillips, Richard Walters, Paul Bawden, Jimmy Matthews, Brian Westcott, Robert Wollacott, Michael Kelly, Tracy Alford, John Adams, Pauline Parkhouse.

Music and drama were to feature very strongly during the next thirteen years. Ian Henderson-Begg wrote the Christmas plays which retained the Nativity at the centre, but gave a broader, wider scope to the Christmas story. Each child had a part either on stage or in the band. Chrissy White is remembered by several for the year he played Herod lying at the table in true Roman style eating a large bunch of grapes!

Christmas lunch and parties were an important part of the end of the winter term. The children had to make their own party hats and walk to the village hall wearing them. The Christmas party was held in school and Maralyn Francis, as she was then, remembers the essential ingredient – Pinky and Perky records for the musical games! Father Christmas (played by Everard Howard and John Mortimer amongst others) always came with gifts often in the form of carefully chosen books.

As part of the summer activities a musical play was devised involving the whole school. These plays covered such themes as pollution, recycling and the Exmoor Beast. The children also took part in many charity concerts at the Queens Hall in Barnstaple raising money for local hospices.

One of the most interesting developments in the 1980s was the small schools co-operation. Each school has its own strengths and weaknesses according to the skills and interests of the staff, and to make full use of others' expertise and the limited funds available for equipment, Filleigh, Swimbridge, Umberleigh and Chittlehampton used to link up and ferry children to one of the schools for an intense day on a particular subject. Children would come to Chittlehampton for science and sport and to use the pottery shed which had a potter's wheel and kiln. Most families in the catchment areas probably still have pottery figures, houses, or bowls made at one of these sessions.

SCHOOLS IN THE PARISH

There was a strong emphasis on sport and the school always had football and netball teams to play other schools and take part in the district tournaments. The school entered the 'Run the World' event and Ian Henderson-Begg ran with the children. Other annual events included pancake races on Shrove Tuesday and egg-rolling before Easter when the children brought decorated hard-boiled eggs to roll down the Square in races, and maypole dancing.

There was a fire in the school at four o'clock in the morning on 4 January 1988 caused by an electrical fault which made the news because the Headmaster could not be woken and only heard about it on the local news as he was dressing. Fortunately the noise had woken Debbie Walters next door to School House. Debbie raised the alarm and the police had to get keys from Polly, the caretaker, who lived out of the village and kept very unfriendly guard dogs! In the summer of 1992 Ian Henderson-Begg retired and Keith Lockyer was appointed.

The Government made many changes to education in general and Chittlehampton suffered OFSTED inspections along with all other schools. OFSTED demands a large amount of paperwork to be completed, with policies to be written for every aspect of school life. A great deal of hard work was rewarded with a successful first review. The Government also introduced the 'literacy hour' which is now firmly in place. Children experience reading, listening to and discussing stories every morning. The millennium drew to a close with the introduction of a 'numeracy hour'. What will they come up with next?

Above: *Chittlehampton School 'Run the World' with Headmaster Henderson-Begg, 1986.*

Left to right, standing: Daniel Peters, Katherine Sherwood, Michael Page, Paul Brookman, Neil Phillips, Tracey Heale, Esme Millar, Stephen Snell, Ann Petherick, Claire Shepherd, Ross Howard, Andrew Page, Ian Henderson-Begg (Headmaster), James Holland, Stuart Govier, Sharon Howard, Juliette Francis, Hannah Buckell, Sarah Heale, Gemmima Johnson, Edward Pope, Susie Wheaton, Sarah Page, Jo Tucker, Sarah Millar;

kneeling: Gale Billington, David Page, Topsy Brookman, Patricia Isaac , Gregor Henderson-Begg, Richard Lamont (head down), Craig Lessiter, [   ], Peter Govier, Desmond Sowden, William Hancock, Barry Lessiter, Jon Docherty (?), Paul Phillips.

THE BOOK OF CHITTLEHAMPTON

Umberleigh Primary School

by Maggie Hyland

How much can a photograph tell us? A moment frozen forever and placed in 1927–28 in a frame. A remarkably clear picture shows children at Umberleigh School, eager faces, anxious faces, stern faces (some of the staff) stare out. So many familiar names link the past to the present. How have these lives panned out? Some who read this will know. Grandparents, parents might be in the picture; 'Look, that's Dorothy'. 'Is that Violet?' Most of the boys in the front row look as if their hands are tied behind their backs!

Apart from their clothes, these children don't appear dissimilar from the pupils at Umberleigh School in this millennium year. Full of promise and eager to learn the skills necessary for a full and rewarding life, but school days then were different. The school logbook, 'Regulations as to the School Records' to be kept by the Principal Teacher, falls open at the year 1927–28. It has a scuffed leather spine and the entries, written in a flowing hand and faded ink, record events. We may not learn who fell over in the playground, or who pinched who during assembly, but it does provide a snapshot of the school seventy years ago.

Above: *Umberleigh School, 1927/8.*

Left to right, back Row: Herbert Thomas, Fred Ford, Tom Smith, Ernie Boucher, Bill Pratt, Syd Loosemore, Ronald Murch;

fourth row: Mrs Beer, Hilda Pratt, Violet Yeo, Alvina Murch, Marjorie Boucher, Nora Dunn, Elsie Knight, Emily Yeo, Hilda Walters, Ella Thomas, Dorothy Clarke, Vera Gammon, ? Cooper, Miss Stevens, Millie Pratt;

third row: Roy Mayne, Erwin Pratt, Monica King, Lillian Short, Grace Mayne, Kate Sanders, Dorothy Yeo, Gwen Kingdon, Leslie Dunn, Jim Murch, Joyce Murch;

second row: Joyce Stuckey, Ruth Murch, Josephine Crawford, Joyce Kingdon, Brenda Murch, Mary Coates, Ethel Alford, Freda Loosemore, Gladys Slee, Ena Kingdon, Florrie Murch, Kathleen Murch, Alice Coates;

front row: Gordon Thomas, Bill Kingdon, Donald Webb, Clifford Short, John Knight, Sydney Stevens, Tom Knight, Gordon Stuckey, Douglas Redwood, Herbert Clarke, Raymond Knight, Jack Phillips.

SCHOOLS IN THE PARISH

The previous year, 1926, had concluded with a report from the Board of Education on an inspection of the vegetable and terrace gardens. 'Both gardens would be better for a little reconstruction: the paths and plots need setting out anew and the western end of the larger garden might be brought into better cultivation.'

31 January	*The children have been weighed and measured today.*
4 February	*Miss Crisp, School Nurse, visited and examined the heads of all the children. The attendance has been very poor this week owing to bad colds and influenza. [And so the influenza continued throughout that month, the average attendance recorded at 29.6%. Poor attendance hit the school throughout the year.].*
24 June	*Very poor attendance due to the stormy weather.*
25 July	*Twenty-two children were absent owing to very heavy rain.*
23 September	*The attendance during the week has been low owing to bad colds, whooping cough and rough weather. [Note the time of year! Those lazy, hazy days of summer weren't quite as wonderful as we have been led to believe.].*
4 March	*Manure has been brought for the school gardens. [Many of the entries seem to concentrate on the progress of the school gardens.].*
15 March	*The boys had a gardening lesson this afternoon as the weather was suitable for turning.*
12 April	*The boys have been at garden work during the afternoon.*
13 April	*The boys have again been at work in the garden. [The boys seem to have been gardening or playing football most afternoons. There is no record of what the girls were up to.].*
4 July	*The boys were very disappointed this morning to find that a pig had broken into their garden during the weekend from an adjoining field and destroyed some of their crops. A report was sent to the Correspondent who kindly came down and saw the damage and undertook to see the owner of the pig. [Who owned that pig? If you think you know, please write to Head Teacher Mrs Adams, Umberleigh School.].*
9 September	*Mr Robins called this morning to see what improvements may be made with regard to the removal of the cinder dump and making of steps down to the lower garden.*
11 September	*The boiler has been inspected today and suggestion was made by the Inspector that two weights be kept on the safety valve instead of four.*

Maybe this is the answer to Umberleigh School's current heating problem! You may recall the school hitting the headlines in 1999. Indoor winter temperatures hit the low point on most winter afternoons, and children and staff had to wear hats and coats in order to keep warm. Mrs Adams was featured on national news. Would the school be closed? Would the children be sent home and parents inconvenienced? Mrs Adams was firm. Only as the last resort. Well we didn't get any additional heating but Mrs Adams became a celebrity with late, late-night shopping at Tesco's, her only hope of anonymity!

Life at Umberleigh School wasn't all gardening, football, boilers, boils, whooping cough, influenza and bad weather in those days:

17 March	*The notice re Scholarships and Free Places has been received, explained to the children and posted in the school.*
20 June	*Notice has been received that Christine Murch has been awarded a Free Place at Crediton High School as the result of the recent Scholarship Examination [which shows what the girls were up to while the boys were titivating the gardens].*
10 February	*Steady and painstaking work was noticed in both classes and the general attitude of the children reflected this. They were anxious to respond and were able to reproduce the main outlines of the Bible Stories taken. The practical and moral application is kept well in view and the tone of the school is an indication of the care that has been taken in Religious Instruction.*

Stand sometime in the car park below the school playground. When the children come out to play the air fills with shouts and laughter. They still play hopscotch, skipping, football and occasionally cats cradle and conkers in the autumn. So the clothes are different but raise a glass to pupils, staff, governors, health workers, kitchen staff, parents and all those associated with Umberleigh School past and present. I'm off to check the valves on that boiler!

Top: *A school gardening group.*

Above: *Umberleigh School in 1953.*

Left to right, back row: Miss Friday, Rachel Murch, Evelyn Cann, Hazel Pratt, Janet Down, Ann Murch, Pat Hill, Sandra Passmore, Lorna Murch, Miss Stephens;

third row: John Andrew, Gordon Gatting, William Passmore, Elizabeth Murch, Denise Alford, Pam Hill, Monica Isaac, Peter Martin, Wilfred Ashelford, Michael Martin;

second row: Andrew Alford, Geoffrey Sharpe, [   ], Elizabeth Rodd, Lorna Friend, Marilyn Passmore, Susan Churchill, Christine Underhill, Terry Hookway, [   ], John Stuckey;

front row: Michael Passmore, Victor Harris, Stephen Tossel, John McCready, Michael Hosking, John Cann, David Gullick, David McCready.

Above: *Certificate presentation, 1976. In April a certificate of merit awarded to Chittlehampton Primary School by the South West Regional National Savings Educational Committee, for outstanding support of the savings movement, was presented to the school's head girl, Sallie Slape, by the District Commissioner, Mr R Speed. Records before 1941 were destroyed by bombing, but since that year the school has saved £26,605.*

Left to right, back row: Mr Baylis, Monica Phillips, Alison Pincombe, William Napier, Grant Oatley, Christopher Adams, Winston Thorne, Louise Halsey, Paul Bawden, Lynn Reed, Monica Needs, Erica Dyson, Anna Tamas, Tracy Alford, Gary Phillips, Richard Walters, Darren Drew, Gary Adams;

Front row: Tamar Tamas, Rebecca Wingrove, Maureen Hammett, Rhonda Fuller, Alison Matthews, Mr Speed, Sallie Slape, Pauline Parkhouse, Dean Sheath, Mark Nichols, Keith Turner, Julia Sedwell.

Below: *Maypole dancing with Headmaster Keith Lockyer in Chittlehampton Square, 1998.*

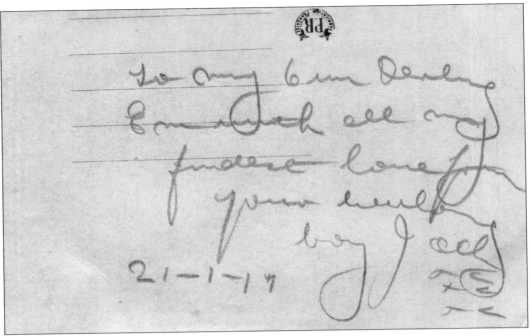

Jack Lethbridge's card to his fiancée in January 1917.

Above: *Postcard sent from A J (Jack) Lethbridge who was fighting in France.*

Above: *Postcard sent to Jack from fiancée Emily.*

Wars

In war, resolution;
in defeat, defiance;
in victory, magnanimity;
in peace, goodwill.

Winston Churchill 1874–1965

The first clear parish record of one of its sons at war is seen on the gravestone of Peter Facey of Gambuston who served at the Battle of Waterloo, that last great crushing defeat of Bonaparte in 1815. Little is known of him, or of any others who left to fight as infantrymen or sailors. He died in 1844 and is buried behind the east window of the church. In the words of Revd Andrew:

In 1901 khaki uniform appeared for the first time in the church, two men being on leave from Aldershot before embarking for South Africa... it was a foretaste of what was to happen a few years later when the Great War of 1914-18 took so many parishioners.

Another extract from his excellent book reads:

Mr James Goss, who was one of the first Reservists to be called up at the commencement of hostilities in South Africa, arrived home on Wednesday night. His coming had not been made known, otherwise a different reception would have been accorded him. A merry peal on the church bells was the first intimation of his arrival to the villagers about 9.30 p.m. Everyone was glad to know that he was safely home. Mr Goss was with General Buller in his stiff task of relieving Ladysmith and he cannot speak too highly of his generalship. He has been in South Africa for two years and his time as a Reservist has now expired. Mr Goss speaks very highly of the Devon's Chaplain (Rev. M Drake), whose father at one time was Vicar of Chittlehampton.

North Devon Journal Herald
24 October 1901

Accursed be he that first invented war

Christopher Marlowe 1564–1593

Chittlehampton sent 144 men to the Great War of 1914. Twenty five were killed and their names are inscribed on the Roll of Honour in the church and on the war memorial in the churchyard.

...There shall be
In that rich earth a richer dust concealed;
A dust whom England bore, shaped, made aware,
Gave, once, her flowers to love, her ways to roam,
A body of England's, breathing English air,
Washed by the rivers, blest by suns of home.

From Rupert Brooke's 'The Soldier', 1914.

Right: *The war memorial in Chittlehampton churchyard.*

THE BOOK OF CHITTLEHAMPTON

Talking with Joan Barrow about her memories of wartime

Above: *Peter Facey's headstone.*

Mr and Mrs Barrow lived all their married lives in Chittlehampton, though they have moved now to South Molton. My grandparents, Emily and Christopher Lethbridge, lived at Ashleigh Villas, Chittlehampton. My grandfather was employed by the Rolle Estate as a mason. He was born in the village, Emily was born at Pilton in Barnstaple. They married on 21 February 1882. Christopher was a member of St Hieritha's Church choir for fifty years, also captain of the ringers for many years. They left the village in 1921 to live at Torrington, both of them are buried here at Chittlehampton. They had five sons and one daughter.

The eldest son, Christopher Frederick (Fred) was also captain of the ringers and taught young men of the village the art of church bellringing. He emigrated to Canada then returned to live again at Chittle-hampton. The other four sons all served in the First War.

Harry worked at Langaton for Mr Jones, farmer, when he left school, then he emigrated to Canada and settled in Winnipeg. When the First War began he joined the 90th Winnipeg Rifles, Canadian Expeditionary Force. In April 1915 he was in Ypres when the Germans first used gas against the Canadians. He was severely wounded in his left leg and foot, gassed, and taken prisoner. In June 1915 his parents were told of his injuries and that he was a prisoner at Palerborn, Westfaler in Germany. In October 1915 he was among exchanged wounded men who landed at Tilbury and were taken to a military hospital at Wandsworth, London. In April 1916 Harry was sent home to Chittlehampton where he received a hero's welcome. After the war he returned to Canada.

Frank, the third son, was in the regular Army with the 3rd Battalion Coldstream Guards. He was killed in action in the first month of the war at Landrecies, France, where he is buried. Frank was killed on 29 August 1914, he was to be married in September 1914. His bride-to-be never did marry.

Arthur John (Jack) was my father. He wanted to work with horses, so on leaving school he worked at Hudscott as a groom. Leaving Hudscott he joined the regular Army. Still wanting to work with horses he joined the Cavalry, 19th Queen Alexandra's Own Royal Hussars. He must have done several spells of duty in France from 1915–17, we have many lovely silk postcards sent from 'Somewhere in France' during those years. In 1919 he was in Germany. At some time early in the war he was billeted at Horfield Barracks, Bristol. While there he met my mother who lived at Westbury-on-Trym. By the spring of 1920 he had left the Army but was still on the reserves. In April of that year they were married and settled down together at Garth Cottage, East Street, Chittlehampton, a very short distance from his

Above: *Arthur John Lethbridge on Dimple.*

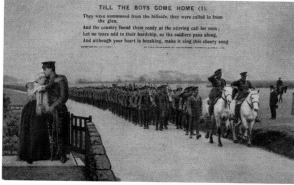

Silk cards and postcards from the First World War – by kind permission of Joan Barrow.

Poster courtesy of Cobbaton Combat Collection

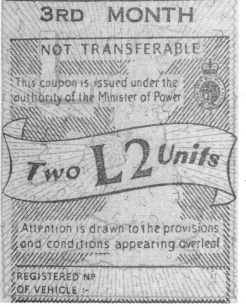

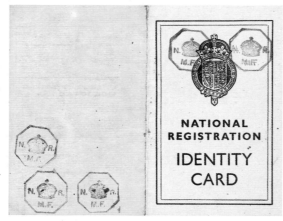

Some interesting wartime paraphernalia.

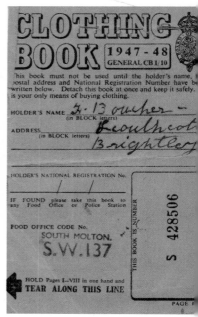

Above: *Jack Lethbridge with fiancée Emily Press in 1919.*

Below right: *May Lethbridge, c.1941.*

parents, Emily and Christopher. The cottage was owned by Lord Clinton who employed him as a mason. He lived there and did the same job until he died in 1954. In 1923 he was appointed clerk and sexton of St Hieritha's Church and held the post for thirty years.

Archie, the fifth and youngest son, emigrated to Canada and, like Harry, settled in Winnipeg. In 1914 he joined the 43rd Battalion Cameron Highlanders of Canada as a scout sniper and was wounded twice. Archie returned to Canada when the war was over.

Chittlehampton, like all towns and villages over England, must have been a very sad place through those war years with the terrible news coming from the front line. People like my grandparents must have known such fear, anxiety and dread when the postman or a telegram arrived.

I have visited battlefields, cemeteries and memorials in the River Somme area, also Ypres and Passchendaele, seeing the thousands of white headstones and huge memorials to 'The Missing'. You realise what a tragic waste of young lives it was.

My nephew, Richard Lethbridge from Chittlehamholt, has a hobby reading local news from old editions of the *North Devon Journal* and the *Western Times* at Barnstaple Library.

Occasionally he reads bits about Chittlehampton, our family, or the war, which he passes on to me.

Moving on a few years, the Second World War again saw my family doing their bit for our country. Archie, still living in Canada, joined the Queen's Own Cameron Highlanders in September 1939 as Company Sergeant Major, arriving in England in December 1939. In May 1943 he went to North Africa with the British 8th Army, then later served in the Italian Campaign.

My father was a sergeant in the local Home Guard. My sister, May Lethbridge who still lives in Chittlehampton, was the first female volunteer from the village, joining the WAAFs in 1941. As LACW Lethbridge, May was mentioned in dispatches for devotion to duty and was awarded an Oak Leaf medal.

Chris Lethbridge, my brother, joined the regular Army in 1946 with the REME, also as a paratrooper with the 16th Independent Parachute Brigade, serving in Germany and Cyprus, and was the last to leave Palestine in 1948.

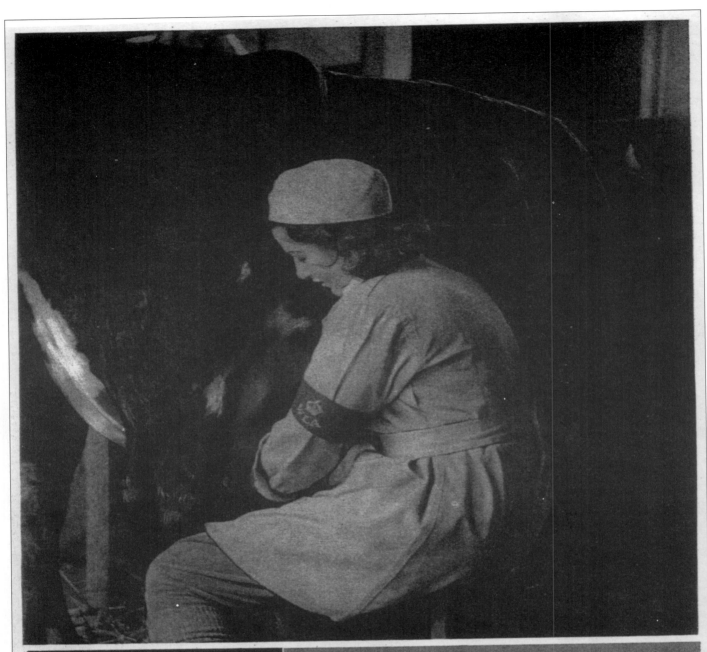

FOOD COMES FIRST

Join the WOMEN'S LAND ARMY and WIN THE BATTLE FOR BREAD

Apply Fairpark Lodge, Fairpark Road, Exeter.

Printed by Fosh & Cross Ltd., London

War came again in 1939 and this time only forty five men left to fight. Four were killed and they have joined those names in the churchyard on the memorial. Agriculture was a reserved occupation – men were commanded to stay and work the land for the War Effort. Evacuees arrived in North Devon – some with their mothers, some without, and all needing help, comfort, food and shelter.

Talking with John Hosking about his remembrance of war in the village.

John Hosking lived and worked all his life at Hawkridge until his retirement. He and his wife, Valerie, now live just outside Chittlehampton.

In the springtime during the war, Arthur and Jane Arscott from Deptford Farm, Umberleigh, were looking for a goose that was laying somewhere down by the stream and Mrs Arscott found a hole in the ground about 100 yards from the house where a bomb had dropped. After they had finished their work the whole family stayed with Arthur's brother, Eddy, sleeping the night and just coming back and doing the necessary work for a few days before they dug the bomb out.

I remember the land mine that dropped at Langaton Farm, in Chittlehampton, which took all the power from the village. At the time we were at Moor Farm, Umberleigh (Bill Arscott's), with my family at a card party. The oil lamp suddenly flared up and the blinds went up and everybody was scared and panicked and the men went out in the yard because they thought it had dropped outside and we children were forbidden to go out. I remember it very well, it was quite a bang. I must have been about eight or nine.

We had two evacuees at Hawkridge and I think they were six and seven. They each had a gas mask and a label around their neck and they came in and had a cup of tea and something to eat. Each had a postcard to write home... The eldest came from the East End of London and the other from Luton. They went to school at Chittlehampton. There were another two that came to Ford Mill and they were about fourteen and fifteen. They used to walk to Barnstaple of a Saturday morning [about six miles] and were very poor. They were old enough to do jobs and used to come up to Hawkridge... my father would give them a bit of pocket money for helping out on the farm.

Some of the parents heard that evacuees were being mistreated and one night in the middle of winter we were playing by the fire in the front room when there was a knock on the door and it was one of the evacuee's fathers. He had heard all these stories and had come on the hop expecting to catch us out. When he saw how happy they were he broke down and wished he hadn't come.

I remember the dog fight over the village with one of our fighters and a German one. I think both aircraft came down. I am not quite sure about this, but I think the German is buried in High Bickington churchyard. I remember just before D-Day when they were practising – they would send convoys of tanks, armoured vehicles and all kinds of equipment around the back roads and I've known them stretch from Kewsland (that is above the hill from Emmett Farm), to Umberleigh nose to tail.

Miska Pulpher came to Chittlehampton as a 12-year-old evacuee in 1941. She sent this picture several years later to the Murch family with whom she had stayed.

In the years when our Country

was in mortal danger

FREDERICK THOMAS BOUCHER

who served 9th JUNE 1940 to 31st DECEMBER 1944

gave generously of his time and

powers to make himself ready

for her defence by force of arms

and with his life if need be.

George R.I.

THE HOME GUARD

After the war the biggest thing that happened was that everything came off ration and you could take the dimmers off the lights of the cars. It was all a gradual process and yet it was exciting really because the war was over and there was a new Government and things to look forward to. The war followed the great depression years of the 1930s. From the farming point of view after the war everything became more and more mechanised.

Talking with Rosemary Peters about her evacuation from Surrey during the Second World War

I was born in Lambeth in the East End of London and lived there until I was about three and a half and think then we moved to Clapham. From there we moved to Surrey where I stayed until I was fourteen. My mother was widowed at thirty four with four of us under twelve. She had a big breakdown so I had to be mother and father to the children. I used to go to school two days and stay home three to look after the baby, so I was used to washing nappies and everything else at a very early age. I used to cycle up to the library when we lived in Surrey and very often the siren would go and you would have to go quietly to the nearest shelter because otherwise you were in trouble. When you used to go to school in the morning and see the empty desks you did not need to ask where everybody was because they had been killed the night before. I lost heaps of school friends like that. Before the doodle bugs we had quite near bombings which used to happen; I think if the Germans had any bombs left they would jettison them over Surrey on the way home. So we had the worst of it. I was nine when the war broke out and spent most of my school life down the shelters doing lessons because you could not do anything else. It was a wonder I had any education at all but I scraped through life and haven't done too bad. I think my mother found it very hard once my father had died to raise the four of us, she just didn't have any money at all because there was no Social Security like today. I think there was parish pay but very little and [one] had to be means tested.

I started work in an insurance office at fourteen and when I came home from work one day Mother said 'We are moving'. We had the chance to be evacuated. Smaller children from the East End were more or less forced to be evacuated and you used to see pictures in the paper of them crying. When the four of us moved, my youngest sister was only a year old, and my brother was a year younger than me and my other sister was four years younger. We didn't know where our destination would take us and got on the train at Paddington with a host of others. We could only bring one suitcase between five of us and one toy... because space was so limited. They fed us on the train and we had a gas mask around our necks and a label on our coats. We stopped at various places. Some went to Wales and some went to the middle of England. The reason we left was because of the bombs called doodle bugs that were dropping towards the end of the war and apparently people were saying if you wanted to be evacuated you could be. We were the last to get off the train and landed up at South Molton where a big coach was waiting to pick us up and they said we were going to a village and ended up in Chittlehampton Square.

There were thirty of us altogether, of various ages, not many big children of my age, only about six of us. Some only stayed a matter of weeks, especially those children from the East End because the country was all new to them and they could not settle down.

We had a direct hit on the houses where we used to live and lost everything a few months after we came down here. Our neighbour's husband died and her children were very badly cut with flying glass.

We slept the first fortnight in the Methodist school room on straw mattresses and the WVS and WI used to feed us a meal every day. They then gave my mother the cottage which is now the village shop but they wouldn't let me stay there; I had to be billeted out because I was older and got sent to a small farm holding at Blakewell and hated it. The owners were both working and I was left with the lodger who never spoke to me and I stayed a fortnight and ran away and came back to the cottage with my mother. I was able to get a job in South Molton and hated it. It was hand sewing rings on tents for soldiers. I stayed there for a while then when my mother's bomb damage money came through she bought me a bicycle. I was sixteen so I got a job in Banbury's as a cashier and stayed there until I was married at just over eighteen... I met Gordon when I was fifteen... we had three children and lived down at Woodlands.

Umberleigh, Atherington, Yarnscombe and Alverdiscott Home Guard, 1940.

© Knight Photographic

Left to right, back row: Henry Kent, Reg Bright, Ron Ashford, Stan Guard, John Knight, George Eastman, Tom Glass, Cliff Glover, John Beer, Fred Folland, Sid Stevens, Bill Seague, Frank Andrews;

fourth row: Ern Smith, Roy Fennell, John Woolacott, Bill Huxtable, Ron Moore, Archie Johns, Arthur Kent, Jack Lee, Bert Hill, Bert Coleman, Fred Williams, Gus Brown;

third row: Jimmy Murch, Frank Beer, Sid Loosemore, Albert Moore, George Stuckey, Fred Boucher, Fred Snow, Claude Johns, Les Street, George Setherton, Percy Jewell, Archie Johns, John Guard;

second row: Bill Rudd, Erne Clayworthy, Albert Kift, Fred Loosemore, Erne Summerville, Cyril Sharp, Charlie Alford, Fred Ford, George Ashford, Jack Courtney, Sid Samson;

front row: Herbert Thomas, Vic King, Archie Woolacott, Percy Squires, Bill Snow, Harry Clarke, Jack Joslin, Gordon Thomas, Ken Fennall, Jack Phillips.

Gordon worked on the farm then we moved to Blackmantle and stayed there for forty years before coming up to the village. Farm pay was £4.10s. a week. A loaf of bread was 4.½d. and a pint of milk 4.½d. and a hundred weight of coal was 3s.9d. Nobody craved for things then like they do today and I think it was probably a better world even if you were ever so hard up, but I don't think I would want to go back to it. We had no water or electricity down at Woodlands and the bath was a tin one in front of the fire and oil lamps and flat irons to do the ironing.

When you think about it we were happy as can be with nothing. I remember when I came to Chittlehampton there were a few quaint old characters. Bessie Upton, a little tiny woman who walked about with no coat in winter or summer and her sleeves rolled up her arms.

There was also a man called Phillips who lived in the house opposite the shop and he and the man next door, who was Margaret Short's father, used to sit on the steps smoking their pipes. Also Audrey Bowden's granny, Rose Turner, who used to be the caretaker up at the school. They all seemed to take to us very well and I think I'm now accepted as a Devonian. My mother has never been back to Surrey but after we moved and could afford it, I went back and actually saw the place where we lived because it was rebuilt exactly the same. I've got a friend who I started school with... and I go up there and stay... Mum never wanted to go back.

A little taste of what it was like in the Home Guard. Fred Glover was a young member at Umberleigh

I was born at Okehampton. My father was at Meldon Quarry and got transferred to Chapelton. We came down and lived next to the Sawmills and I used to cycle up from there to the Home Guard at Umberleigh. Our drill hall was in the Umberleigh village hall which was then situated between the Rising Sun and Ford Cottages in the quarry.

There were five Home Guard sections in our company which included High Bickington, Filleigh, Chittlehampton and West Buckland School (the senior class). West Buckland were really good

soldiers and were already trained in shooting. We did most of our training in Chittlehampton Square. There were seventy of us in the Home Guard at Umberleigh with about twenty of the older ones and fifty youngsters. It was mostly labourers and farmers' sons. We all had our own shotguns and then they issued us with rifles and we had to go to Filleigh to learn how to shoot. Then we had a Lewis gun which is a light machine-gun and got really expert with it.

When I went in the Army they gave us the Bren gun which was the only one the British Army had at that time. They didn't think we could handle it. I was based in Glasgow where I did my initial training and one day we had a sweepstake because we were all good shots. We had to fire fifty rounds... and the one who had the most rounds would win the sweepstake. I had thirty five bulls out of fifty because of the machine-gun practice I had in the Home Guard.

The church parades on Sundays consisted of marching from Umberleigh to Atherington. In those days we had leaders like Churchill and Montgomery and they all realised that if we were going to win the war it had to be with God's help; but nowadays they try to run it without Him and then they are in a mess. In those days Montgomery never went into battle without a prayer-meeting with his officers and that's the most important thing that I remember in the Home Guard. I was almost three years in it and everyone that completed this length of time had a Defence Medal. In the Home Guard we used to do guard duty during the week. My night was Thursdays with a dozen of us guarding Umberleigh Road, the railway bridge and the timber yard which had thirty thousand pounds worth of wood they put there in the war to keep it from being burnt up... One night on patrol we lost a couple of chaps and eventually they were found asleep on a binder in Murch Bros. shed. At that time it wasn't locked up.

Major Samford, an ex-Army officer, was in over-all charge of us. He lived at Filleigh. In charge of us at Umberleigh was Mr Snow, the station master, and second-in-command was a chap called Clarke that lived in Atherington School House. We used the Army lorries which came from the nearest unit to pick us up to go anywhere, the rest of the time we walked if we were just going to Filleigh... There were no cars and the farmers only had their tractors.

Chittlehampton Home Guard.

Left to right, back row: Jack Matthews, Desmond Peters, Dick Wythe;
third row: Harry Latham, Bert Phillips, Percy Wheaton, John Sussex, Denzil Waldron, Arthur Lean;
second row: Harold Smoldon, Harold Grimshire, Bill Smoldon, Wilfred Matthews, Arthur Parkhouse, Jack Nott;
front row: Bill Johns, Fred Matthews, Sgt. Jack Lethbridge, Major Michael Cardus, Keeper Judy, Keeper Pugsley,
Jack Thorne and the photographer assistant's dog.

The people of Umberleigh were very kind to us in many ways. When we were out all night they would come out with a jug of tea.

Desmond Peters talks about his time in the Chittlehampton Home Guard

One night we had to go into South Molton and guard it. Every road had to be manned and you had to stop everybody. There weren't many people about then and they had to give their name. It was a load of old rubbish really. There were three of us at the top of North Street where you go down to Haache Lane. It was a lot of old farce really and in the evening we were sat down having a fag and someone came along and we were scared stiff. We decided it was a man coming, anyway Lionel Philips jumped out with his rifle up and this was a laugh in the Home Guard for a long time when he said 'Halt! who cometh thither?

After so long in the Home Guard you had a bayonet to put on your rifle and they encouraged us to do exercises at home. When it came to the next meeting Sid Ashford came in without his bayonet and he said 'I was doing my exercises at home and it went up through the ceiling and I couldn't get it down.' It was all a laugh really. I know we were only youngsters but it didn't seem to be taken seriously. One night there was a bit of excitement. A German plane went up through the main street of Chittlehampton with a Spitfire behind him, peppering him, which brought him down in Roborough Moor.'

Percy Wheaton was also in the Chittlehampton Home Guard

I was born at Mile House, Chittlehampton. The headquarters for the Home Guard was behind the Bell Hotel in the skittle alley; there was also a galvanised shed in which to keep the explosives and so on. We used to do our drilling in the Square and go up to Abbots Hill for rifle practice, lying on the ground and shooting up against the hedge with someone put out in the other side of the field to make sure no-one came up. We also went to Filleigh on the range a good many times. A little way back from Heddon Cross there used to be a quarry and we used to go in and throw hand grenades in over. I remember once going down there with Umberleigh, Filleigh and

South Molton Home Guards throwing these grenades and one chap let the spring go and still had it in his hand and they shouted to him and he dropped it and someone just managed to pick it up and throw it out over or else there would have been a serious accident. Of course they were live and you only had four seconds, when the spring went you had to let it go. Some Sundays we would go into the cinema in Barnstaple and Terraneus Tours of South Molton would take us in to see some war films.

Once we had to go into South Molton to a mock attack. Our lot came in going across the fields down beside the cemetery wall in over the cattle market and through. A lot of us had double-barrel guns with blanks. Filleigh attacked from the other side coming in by the back of the hospital. They knocked on the door of a house and asked to go through, and came out at the back of the Post Office behind the South Molton Home Guard who were lying down with their machine-guns! We came in across the fields and two or three girls were out there. When they saw us they ran and told them in the town that we were coming in that way. Nobody came across the fields to capture us; instead they sent several of their men up the road and by that time we were in South Molton shooting. They said it wasn't fair us coming across the fields.

One night we were all woken up at one o'clock and told that the Germans were coming, but it was just training. When we were attacking South Molton there were several of the Army chaps taking notes. South Molton had some good shooters. When we were on manoeuvres Arthur Littlejohns and Bert Phillips were two dispatch riders in our platoon to take messages on to the next Home Guard. In the photograph... of our group there was a dog that Jack Thorne had on his lap which belonged to the photographer. Not everyone was present on the day the photograph was taken so there are some missing.

I was in the Bell when the land mine dropped and all of a sudden the lights went out followed by a bang and the place shook. The searchlight soldiers were in the pub at the time and we knew it was a bomb and started singing to take people's minds off it. Mrs Lock, the landlady, said: 'Shut up, they will hear you!' The same night I went over and saw the crater, it was four or five feet deep.

A Victorian Daughter of the Parish

Brenda Murch's story is one that demonstrates, with unaffected charm, all those ideals of family life as well as their practical application. Her healthy determination to grow and to explore independently shows the degree of freedom a happy and secure childhood can provide. She was a young woman alone in the early part of the last century when she set out for Botswana in South Africa, and she chose New Zealand for her retirement. She wrote a brief memoir for her niece Catherine (Pat Murch's daughter), which finishes abruptly with her appointment as midwifery sister in the maternity department of the Charing Cross Hospital. Some time after that she served as nursing sister in London's Holloway Prison.

Later she joined Queen Elizabeth's Colonial Nursing Service, and went to South Africa, becoming matron of Lobatis Hospital in what was then Botswana. It was here that her great service was recognised, and she was awarded the MBE. During the Royal Tour of South Africa she was presented to King George VI. After her retirement in the 1960s, Brenda Murch married for the first time, though sadly she was widowed after only four years. In 1967 she went to join her half sister Ruth Heathcoat in New Zealand. There, at the age of 77, she married again, and became Brenda Carling. She died in New Zealand at the age of 93. Her nephew Pat tells of her rich life, and how, though living so far away in New Zealand, she retained close ties with her family.

'I was born on 20 August 1897 at Pitt House, Umberleigh, North Devon, in the parish of Chittlehampton. The house had been built by a Mr Olgavy who cut the North Devon railway. It was a modern house with indoor water sanitation (which in those days was rare) with a pull-up release instead of a pull-down chain. The house was later converted into two cottages.

I do not remember my mother who had died when I was about eighteen months old. My brother, Leonard, was five years older than I and at school, so that I had a lonely childhood except for the company of my dog, a liver and white spaniel called Bruce. I was very fond of Bruce. When he and I had reached the age of ten years he was killed by the express train. He had become very deaf. That was a very sad day for me.

We had four boy cousins; Jim, Frank, Albert and Walter (who lived at Umberleigh) and my brother Leonard spent a lot of time with them and they spent days with us too and were very caring for me. Their mother, who was my Aunt Lucy, had trained them to take care of me because I had no mother. I was always well cared for by either a housekeeper or servant girl. Bruce and I spent most of our days rambling in the fields or through Pitt Wood. I knew no other children and met very few people, my Dad being the most important fellow in my life. He was an agricultural engineer and his work was among the farming community, whom he met chiefly at the market towns of Barnstaple, Bideford and South Molton, and in later years at the local market at Umberleigh.

I loved my Dad very much and I would walk through Pitt Wood (with Bruce) to meet him as he walked from Umberleigh Station. I would then be hoisted onto his shoulder for the ride home. That was also my mode of travel to Blakewell Chapel on Sundays and I still remember the big worry it was to me not to knock Dad's bowler hat off.

I lived a healthy outdoor life and met no other children until, at about six years of age, I commenced school at Chittlehampton – a two-and-a-half mile walk.

It was a few years before my friend Winnie joined me on our road to school and we became and remained friends for the remainder of her life. There were two boys also taking the same road to school so we had our share of tough teasing.

I was seven years old when we left Pitt and went to live at Umberleigh; Winnie had to walk from Brightley Mill making her school walk three-and-a-half miles, but she didn't have to milk the cows as I did from the age of ten years.

Top: *Brenda's half brothers and sisters, c.1920.*
Lloyd, Harry, Bernard, Christine, Ruth, Alvina and Ronald.

Below: *A H Murch and his second wife Alice with young Lloyd and Harry at Dorridge in 1913.*

Our housekeeper at that time was Mrs Eastlake and she was the eighth housekeeper I could remember. When I was ten years old Dad met and married a young wife. It was a happy marriage and soon after we left Umberleigh and went to live at Dorridge, where the second family was born. I was twelve years old when Harry was born and he was the first boy I had ever had anything to do with; I thought he was wonderful. He was, too, a beautiful chubby little boy. I was still at Dorridge and at school when Lloyd was born. At the age of fourteen years I left school and went to live with Aunt Selina and Uncle Bill (Murch), a move which had been planned by Dad and Uncle Bill some time before, but I worked between the two homes. Aunt Selina always sent me to Dorridge when a new baby was expected or at pig-killing time. I was seldom idle and had three cows to milk at Umberleigh and take to and from Nethercleave, where we had two fields and an orchard. My Umberleigh work comprised milking and dairy work, serving in the shop and anything else that came along – a general factotem.

People came to the shop from a wide area, the community and gentry, there was no other store in the neighbourhood and business was good, no cars on the roads in those days. We usually had four men in the house; Uncle Bill and three men in the room up the back stairs (two worked at Murch Bros.) and the junior railway porter lived with us too.

Barnstaple was our market town where Aunt Selina always went on Friday market day to stock up the perishables. Our dry goods were delivered by dealers from Bideford and Barnstaple and Aunt Selina's shop was a very busy little centre. Customers came from a wide area, there was no regular closing time and often in the summer months we would be busy in the shop up to ten o'clock.

The First World War had started in 1914 and many of the boys from the surrounding parishes had enlisted – later there was conscription. From our family Frank Murch was on munitions and so were Frank and Leonard. I think they went to Gillingham in Kent. Leonard and Walter were exempt on account of the work they were doing. There was a dearth of lads and those of us young folk left tended to stick together.

Aunt Selina was also an egg dealer and another of my tasks was to collect eggs from the surrounding poultry keepers, and this was quite heavy work as a basket of eggs can be weighty. I then had to test every egg. Our method of testing was to have a box with a candle burning in it. Opposite the flame was an egg-sized hole. An egg was held before it and if it was clear the egg was good; but if there was a shadow it was not a fresh egg. The depth of the shadow indicated how fresh the egg was and whether or not it could be sent to the dealer, usually not. I had to pack the eggs in egg boxes, label the boxes, fasten them and take them to the station to rail them to the egg dealer at Southampton. I remember there was much trouble about broken eggs by the time the boxes reached Southampton.

As a teenager I began to take a second look at the few boys who were left, but I was hard to please and never did find the right one, not in my youth or later. We young folk walked round in groups; pairs had already been split up due either to the forces or munitions.

There were food shortages and it was quite a long time after the war ended before we could forget food rationing; keeping the local store and trying to please all the customers was quite a nightmare.

I spent ten years with Aunt Selina and Uncle Bill and when Aunt Selina was ready to retire from her shop I was given the opportunity to take it over, but I declined, the main reason being that I had an urge to see more of the world than I'd seen in North Devon. My Aunt and Uncle understood, as did my parents. I was unsure as to how I would start out in 1923. There was a cousin at Croydon of whom I was fond, so I went to spend a fortnight's holiday with her and her husband – Stan and Florrie Griffiths. Florrie had done nursing and she suggested that I enter the nursing world and she helped me to get started as I knew nothing about applying to be accepted for training. We bought the *Nursing Mirror* and applied to three different hospitals for application forms. The difficulty was that a Secondary School Certificate was required. My school education had been acquired at Chittlehampton School and as the village was at the top of a hill I could truthfully write that I was educated at Chittlehampton High School!

Above: *Brenda Murch's father, Albert Henry (A H) Murch.*

My application was accepted and I remained there until my training was completed and I was a State Registered Nurse. I was asked to join the trained personnel as Staff Nurse, this I did and remained at the hospital until November 1927.

Our Matron advised all her nurses to get a second certificate after SRN; either fever, children or midwifery. I decided on midwifery and applied and was accepted as a pupil midwife at the East End Maternity Hospital in Commercial Road, London E1. It was a six month training hospital district. We were a happy staff and I quite enjoyed my training for the Certificate of the Central Midwives Board, especially the district work which enabled me to see how the poor of London lived. A one-room home with often four or five children, and if it was a night delivery and the children were at home, we had to screen them behind a hanging sheet. We became well acquainted with Dockland and were never out of sight of policemen. I have heard that many of this type of London slum were wiped out by the bombs which fell during the 1940–45 [sic] war. It was while I was waiting for CMB exam results that I went to Bristol and did some private nursing and while there I was called

home to Umberleigh because Uncle Bill was failing and wanted me. I stayed with Uncle Bill until he passed on, which was quite soon. I was so sad to lose him, we had been good pals and had a lot of fun. Aunt Selina was in good health and did not need me to remain at home with her, so I returned to nursing. I applied and was accepted as a midwifery sister at the maternity department of the Charing Cross Hospital, where we were training medical students and third-year nurses of that hospital for the CMB exam.

I had applied for and been granted the Government allowance for midwives who would undertake to teach midwifery for two years after obtaining their certificate. I had received no salary during my own midwifery training, but we were entitled to meals and accommodation. It was a lean six-month period, but we could get theatre tickets from Matron and we walked a lot.

(Brenda Murch's diary finishes here, only part way through a long and useful life. Below we see a remarkable picture of her presentation to King George VI.).

Leisure

As Di Drummond in her contribution says, the leisure pursuits of the parish cover a pretty wide variation. One of the more colourful is everyone's liking for dressing up! Most occasions seem to be an excuse for some very inventive costumes to be paraded, while indoor productions become more lavish and professional. At the end of the 1980s, a group of WI (Women's Institute) widowers, tired of making do while wives were doing Institutely things, began to entertain at the Women's Institute annual parties. Their popularity and success led, in 1989, to the first pantomime performed in Umberleigh's village hall. It was determined then that any proceeds should be towards the three community aspects of the village: Umberleigh School, the Good Shepherd Church and the hall itself, and over about eleven years, the group now known as The Really Useless Theatre Company has made over £10,000 for those three amenities, and has even been able to donate £3,000 to local charities from raffles held at each performance.

Above: *Frances Smoldon and Alice Stone (née Smoldon) outside Upper Biddacott Farm, c.1910.*

Left: *Barnstaple Operatic Society – Dancing Years, 1973. Everard Howard is partnered by Dorothy Horwood, from the Torbay Operatic Society.*

Facing page above: Dame and the Devil *with Barry Alford and Paul Manley.*

Facing page below: *Mayfair, 1942. Included in the picture are: Tony Philips, Ken Peters, Derek Matthews and Michael Trigger.*

LEISURE

Butterfly photographs © Mike Braid

© Cobbaton Photographic

119

Above left: *Fishing on the Taw.*

Above right: *The hunt at Umberleigh – a hand-painted photograph, 1940s.*

Left: *Bailiffs Paul Carter, Roger Bickley and Jeremy Boyd with fish taken in one night from poachers.*

Below: *Church kneeler sewn by Iris Wheaton.*

Above: *Everard Howard sings at the Queens Theatre, Barnstaple.*

Facing page above: *Dads Army at South Molton Carnival.*

Left to right: Jack Phillips, Trevor Martin, Frank Squires (in the turret), Michael Martin, Tim Flavell (with umbrella), Peter Martin, Mike Lyle (on bike), John Webber, Barry Murch, Bev Huxtable, Bill Huxtable.

Facing page below: *St Trinians, the Umberlegh entry at South Molton Carnival.*

Left to right: Nora Belton, Eddie Belton, Ann Headon, Brenda Headon, Patrick Phillips, David Strudwick, [   ], Elaine Reed, Shirley Woolacott, Judith Mayne, Susan Ettery, Margaret Ettery, Diane Murch, Yvonne Headon, Angela Parkhouse, Sylvia Westcott, Pat Delve.

Fêtes at Chittlehampton and Umberleigh 1999

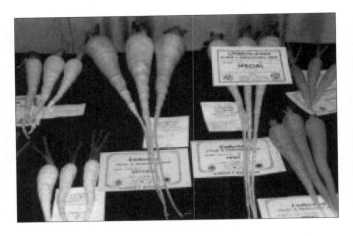

Top: *YFC 'Welly walking'.*

Centre: *Dog Show.*

Bottom: *Pony Event.*

Top: *Vegetable Competition.*

Centre: *Junior Football Competition, Chris Dent in goal.*

Bottom: *Face Painting. These butterflies are Ruth Lockyer and Rebecca Luscombe.*

Chittlehampton Fête, 1999. Ivor Bourne and John Hosking manage the raffle.

Above: *Chittlehampton Women's Institute Club – an outing c.1910. Included in the photograph are Syd Rendle and Farmer Jones and (seated) Mrs Arscott. On her right is Nurse Seeley, and next to her is Alice Smoldon with her sister Francis on the floor in front.*

Below: *Women's Institute, 1950s, with Chittlehampton and members from five neighbouring groups.*

LEISURE

In the closing years of the 19th century, in Ontario, Canada, Adelaide Hoodless' baby died because of contaminated milk. The loss made her determined to teach other women the importance of domestic hygiene, and on 19 February 1897 she founded the Women's Institute.

Eighteen years later, the first Women's Institute in the UK was formed at Llanfairpwll, Anglesey, on 11 September, and the first in Devon was at Cullompton in 1917. The Devon Federation of Women's Institutes was formed on 9 April 1920.

The Chittlehampton WI was formed in 1940 and the ladies met in the Toc H room, now Hope Cottage. A friendship was formed at that time with a WI in New Zealand who sent food parcels throughout the war. This friendship continued until the Chittlehampton WI closed, through lack of members, in 1989, just missing its 50th anniversary. Many members from Chittlehampton now attend the Umberleigh and Atherington Women's Institute which meets in Umberleigh's village hall.

Above: *Chittlehampton Women's Institute, 1966.*

Left to right, back row: Mrs Guard, Mrs Seldon, Mrs Brown, Margery Ford, Mrs Coleman, Rosemary Peters, Louisa (Granny) Peters, Joyce White, Shirley Hooper, Wyn Bayliss;

third row: Mrs Webber, Freda Eastman, Mrs Loosemore, Margery Pinkham, Katie Short, Gertie Matthews, Emily Lethbridge, Emily Knowles, Ruth Buckingham, Mrs Yeo, Florrie Isaac, Doris Jones;

seated: Ida Baker, Ethel Potter, Dawn Phillips, Nanette Peters, Nelly Howard, Vera Dallyn, Sylvia Peters, Rene Waldron, Jean Benn, Mary Glover;

front: Mrs Woolacott, Pat Seldon, Hazel Dallyn, Belle Trigger, Stella Pendleberry, Jayne Bayliss, Lorna Lock.

Butterflies and Birds in the Parish

As several kneelers in the church proclaim, Mike Braid's knowledge and appreciation of butterflies is very considerable indeed. These extracts come from an excellent article he wrote:

Quite the most rare butterfly recorded in Chittlehampton is the Camberwell Beauty, and that was around one hundred years ago. Unfortunately, because it is a very unusual immigrant from the Continent, we will probably never see another here.

Butterflies are one of the most sensitive indicators of environment and are very fussy about their habitat. Probably the first place that people think of as home for butterflies is their garden, and indeed many of the more common species are regular visitors. The Peacock and Small Tortoiseshell are both colourful and frequently seen. They spend the winter as adult butterflies, rather than as caterpillars, eggs or pupae, often in dark corners of sheds or porches. During the summer they may be joined by handsome Red Admirals and Painted Ladies, both immigrants from the South. The Painted Lady originates from North Africa and often arrives in huge numbers.

They all love Buddleia flowers, as do the common Large and Small Whites which are the pests that lay eggs on cabbages! A visitor seen less often is the delicate Holly Blue, which can be spotted around holly trees in May and again in August; its caterpillar feeds on ivy in the winter months and holly in the summer, hence its name. To my mind the real harbinger of spring is the Orange Tip, frequently seen around Chittlehampton in April and May when it is the first butterfly to hatch as distinct from hibernating over winter.

As the year progresses to summer, the Green Veined White appears. It looks rather like a Cabbage White but has heavy veining on its underside and is not interested in cabbages! The Common Blue sits in flowery fields in summer. The Comma with its jagged wings and distinctive white comma mark on a dark underside may be seen as early as April and on and off until the autumn.

The Small Copper with its bright forewings settles in small numbers on field flowers in the summer or on Michaelmas Daisies in the autumn. During late June and July the unimproved grassland fields are full of Meadow Browns and Ringlets, so called because of their ring markings on dark brown wings. In smaller numbers the Small Skipper and Large Skipper can be seen darting from flower to flower, hence their name. In hedgerows the Gatekeeper, like a diminutive Meadow Brown, can be seen in large numbers during July and August.

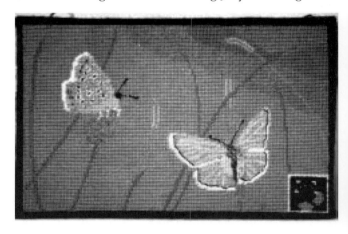

Three more scarce butterflies can be seen in the countryside around Chittlehampton if you are fortunate and observant. The Green Hairstreak is a small brown butterfly which has a bright green underside with a slight white 'hairstreak'. If you are lucky you can see the large, handsome Dark Green Fritillary, with dark green and silver spots on its underside, feeding on a thistle flower or soaring away in the breeze, on the edge of woods or copses and in the open countryside. Its caterpillar feeds on violets. Another migrant from southern Europe most years is the Clouded Yellow. It never seems to sit on vegetation with its wings open to the sun, so it is difficult to see its black on deep-yellow markings.

The last type of habitat found in the Chittlehampton area is woodland. Here the Silver Washed Fritillary is seen in the summer with its silver and green 'washed' underside, sometimes flying along hedgerows and even, very occasionally, I have seen it feeding on Buddleia in my garden. This is a Violet eater like many of the fritillary family. The eggs are laid in a crevice of the bark of oak trees, then they hatch and spend the winter in the crevice, crawling to the ground in the spring to find a violet to feed on, a very haphazard approach! Two less obvious, but very beautiful, butterflies can also be found here: the Purple Hairstreak, so called because of the iridescent purple sheen on its upper wings and distinctive 'hairstreak' on its grey underside, lives and feeds on oak trees. The White Admiral is stunning with blackish upper wings with a white stripe and a pretty grey and brown underside. It is strictly a woodland butterfly and is most easily seen soaring in open spaces in woods and visiting bramble flowers. It is present in two places around Chittlehampton in smallish numbers and these appear to be the only colonies in the North Devon area.

Butterfly Conservation is a charity dedicated to saving butterflies and their habitats. There is a Devon branch which helps manage sites where some of the county's rarest butterflies are found.

When I was a boy I collected butterflies, they seemed so plentiful then. Now I feel they are disappearing too rapidly for all sorts of reasons and we should be helping them to multiply (Cabbage Whites excepted!). Putting them in a glass case is unacceptable to me now. Photographing them, however, is challenging and enjoyable. Let's hope we see many of these attractive insects in good numbers in Chittlehampton for many years to come.

Stephen Cooke and his wife live at the foot of a wooded hill overlooking the River Taw. A mill leat runs through their garden which is over-shadowed by mature Elders and Grey Willows – an ideal situation for bird-watching. He writes:

The common residents – Robin, Blackbird, Song Thrush, Dunnock, Blue Tit, Great Tit, Coal Tit, Chaffinch and Wren – are never far away. The Nuthatch is a frequent visitor to the bird table, as are the Willow Tit and Greenfinch. On two occasions we have had Treecreepers nest behind a post that supports the porch on the house.

A short walk along the road to the Douglas Firs will usually reveal Goldcrests scurrying around the branches in search of small insects. This is our smallest British bird. Across the road the shy but beautiful Bullfinch lives amongst the Willows overhanging the leat, and there too we see the largest member of the thrush family, the Mistle or Storm Thrush, nicknamed because of its habit of singing at the height of a storm. Goldfinches and Long Tailed Tits move around in flocks. We once found a Long Tailed Tit's nest in a small holly bush, one of the most beautiful nests, made of lichen and cobwebs and lined with feathers.

Buzzards soar on thermals high above us and often have squabbles with crows. Rooks probe the field for leather jackets and Magpies and Jays skulk around in the bushes and hedgerows. Tawny Owls can be heard most nights. Both the Green and Great Spotted Woodpeckers are residents of our part of the valley. An occasional Sparrowhawk swoops over the hedges in search of unwary small birds. In contrast, the Kestrel frequently hovers over the railway line with its eyes set on beetles and small mammals. A few years ago we used to see a Barn Owl hunting along the railway line at dusk. Sadly this beautiful and once common bird is now an endangered species due to its loss of nest sites.

The River Taw is home to Mallard ducks from its source to the estuary. Wild Mallards are nervous birds and easily flushed whilst walking the river bank. Dippers are seen on the fast rapids below the weir, constantly bobbing up and down, and another bird always on the move is the Grey Wagtail. Grey Herons wade in shallow water in search of fish and eels to spear with their long, pointed beaks, whilst the cormorant, another expert fisherman, uses a different tactic. Cormorants dive and swim under water to catch fish up to three pounds in weight. After feeding they stand on the riverbank with their wings held open to dry.

Moorhens live on the weir pool. This shy bird rears two or three clutches of chicks each year. No walk along the riverbank is complete without sight of a Kingfisher... usually seen as an iridescent flash, so there is never any doubt over identification.

All the birds so far mentioned are residents, and so may be seen all the year round. In March with lengthening days and warmer weather when many insects hatch, the bird population starts increasing dramatically. This is due to the arrival of summer migrants. One of the first to arrive is the Chiffchaff that announces its presence by repeatedly calling 'chiff chaff chiff chaff chiff chaff'. This small bird is a member of the warbler family. Many warblers are difficult to identify as they are very much alike, they really are LBJs (little brown jobs).

Of the Hirundines (Swallows and Martins) the first to arrive in about the middle of April is the Sand Martin. We have a large colony that wastes no time digging holes in the river bank to make their nests, and this is fortunate as Sand Martins are declining in other areas. Soon after come the Swallows and House Martins, followed in May by the Swift. Swifts are masters of the air; after nesting they don't perch but keep flying day and night until they nest again the following year.

Winter migrants spend the summer breeding and rearing their young in more northerly latitudes. As colder weather sets in they fly south to our warmer climate. Large flocks of Starlings, Redwings and Fieldfares arrive from Scandinavia. In very cold weather when snow smothers the ground, Redwings, normally quite shy, are only too keen to raid the bird table in their quest to stay alive. Hard weather across the country drives Snipe and Woodcock to the West Country in search of unfrozen ground into which they can probe for food with their long beaks.

A duck that is certainly not rare but visits the estuary in thousands is the beautiful little Teal. In hard weather Teal come inland to seek sanctuary in the dead water half a mile up the valley. An estuary bird to be seen these last two winters is the Goosander, a diving duck that swims under water to catch fish. Another diving bird seen recently for the first time is the Little Grebe.

Since the beginning of the Second World War we have seen a tremendous change in farming practice. Horses have given way to tractors, hay meadows that were adorned with wild flowers have given way to high-yielding grass that is forced with nitrogen to provide three cuts a year. Wet meadows have been drained and hedges removed to provide large fields that are more suitable for modern machinery. Oak woodland has been felled and replaced with fast-growing conifers. Pesticides and herbicides are used in vast quantities in the quest to increase yields.

Our agricultural industry should not be blamed for being progressive, it has the tremendous responsibility of feeding the nation. Unfortunately there is a cost which is borne by our wildlife. We cannot turn the clock back but we can do something to help birds. Make a bird table and feed them through the leaner times. Make a variety of nest boxes suitable for birds other than tits. Tolerate untidy overgrown corners; they are a micro habitat for wildlife. Leave a few dead and rotting trees where they stand so that they remain as feeding stations and nest sites for woodpeckers and nuthatches, the sight of them and their song will reward you.

Facing Page, main picture: *Orchids in meadow land at Umberleigh.*

Facing above left: *White Admiral, Chittlehampton, 1997.*

Facing above right: *Meadow Brown, Stowford, 1996.*

Sport

In this parish sport has always been a vibrant part of village life. There is a long history of endeavour, and, indeed, success.

There must be some mention here of the three traditional sports: hunting, shooting and fishing. The Eggesford Hunt meets twice a season at Chittlehampton, and there are enthusiastic followers in the area, but the Devon and Somerset Staghounds, who used to meet at The Bell, no longer do so.

There is no commercial pheasant shoot within the parish, although there is a thriving and well-run syndicate at Emmett.

Roger Bickley, once water bailiff on the River Taw, is now Fisheries Officer of the Taw and its tributaries. Roger writes:

The River Taw is described as one of the best combined salmon and sea trout fisheries in the South West, and is particularly noted for its spring salmon of 10–15lbs, and its large sea trout which also achieve double figures.

Above: *Ross Howard in 1994. Ross had his first success in the Pony Club when he was ten years old. He won fifteen trophies with his horse Timmy. Later on, he became fifth in the world in the Mounted Games and in 1997 became British Pairs Champion.*

Below: *The hunt meets at The Bell in the early 1900s.*

Apart from March when spinning is allowed, all fish are taken on the fly, with names like Willey Gunn and Silver Stoats Tail. Sea trout are caught mainly at dusk or after dark when fishermen often have to share their fishing pool with otters, which have many holts on the Taw in and around Umberleigh.

Fishing permits used to be divided into beats (a stretch of river perhaps half a mile long) which could be purchased for a day from around £25 from the Rising Sun Hotel. These however have been sold to private individuals who now own almost all the fishing rights on the River Taw. A stretch of privately-owned beats known as Riparian Rights, perhaps a mile-long double bank, will fetch around £300,000 in the most sought-after areas.

As well as salmon and sea trout and a few coarse fish (roach and dace), the river at Umberleigh will see elvers (baby eels) moving upstream in March/April to find a good home to grow in (ponds, etc.). Elvers are big business. They are taken out of the river below Newbridge with dip nets and can fetch up to £300 per kilo.

Lampreys, those prehistoric creatures, arrive in June to dig a redd (a hole in the river bed) to lay their eggs and ensure the next generation.

Less welcome are the salmon poachers who net the river any time between February and September. (One night's poached catch of salmon and sea trout is shown on page 128, although Roger is justly proud of his quite legitimate catch of sea trout taken in one night.). The Taw has a long history of poaching. Professional gangs often take fish to supply the London market for special events such as Wimbledon and Ascot.

The 1970s saw the rise of the infamous Bridport Gang, who poached the rivers of the South West as well as Scotland and the River Wye. The falling price of salmon has fortunately made this activity less attractive and deer poaching seems to be on the wain for the same reason.

Below: *Fishing on the Taw.*
Left: *Doctor Augustus Greenwood-Penny 1896–1956*
Right: *Doctor Arnold Saxty Good 1875–1931.*

SPORT

© Roger Bickley

Above: Seat trout and reel – one night's catch on the Taw in 1993.

Cricket and football have long been the best attended of sports, and therefore most written about or recorded. Indoor sports are the more audience restricted (perhaps because quite often they are held in public houses), and for some strange reason, equestrian sports seem not to be much recorded. The fisherman's need for stillness and quiet is perhaps the reason for the lack of much public record (though doubtless the private recounting makes up a good deal for that). Shove ha'penny, skittles, pool and darts are all popular sports in the parish. The South Molton District Darts League was founded in 1956 and has played at The Bell since 1958. In 1961–2 they won the League, the Etonian and Denzil Cups. Stan Harris was Singles Champion, Tony Phillips and Gerald Woolacott were Doubles Champions. Today there is one darts team, two pool teams, two mens' and two ladies' skittle teams. There are also those activities which can be described either as hobbies, or as leisure pursuits.

Below: Fishing in the late 1880s – note the size of the salmon.

Above: *Ladies Skittles Team of 1975 with the landlord Dave Reed.*

Left to right: Cynthia Westacott, Dawn Phillips, Mavis McKeiver, Judy Leach, Evelyn Beer, Margaret White, Liz Slape.

Above left: *Mens' Skittles team in the 1920s.*

Left to right: F Burnett, S Grimshire, F Harris, W G Dean, F Matthews, W Arscott.

Left: *Ladies' Skittles team in 1985.*

Left to right, standing: Pauline Steer, Myra Hobson, Marge Ford, Pam Pickard, Alison Matthews;

sitting: Nicola Smoldon, Liz Slape, Mary Parker, Diane Ballinger

Below left: *Men's Skittles team in 1983.*

Left to right, back: Colin Alford, John Webber;

centre: Bob Ballinger, John Wheaton, Barry Murch;

front: Bob Slape, Fred Hosegood, Chris Parker, David White.

Facing page above: *Ladies' Skittles team in 1968.*

Left to right, standing: Liz Flemming, Pat Delve, Pat Strudwick, Liz Slape, Sylvia Pope, Dawn Phillips;

seated: Marie Davis, Shirley Hooper, Mary White, Margaret White.

Facing page below: *Men's Darts team 1961/2, winners of the Etonian Cup, Denzil Cup and South Molton League Champions.*

Left to right, standing: Frankie Squires, Jack Parkhouse, Ern Ashton, Gordon Lilley, Bernard Michell;

seated: Joe Chapman, Wilf Matthews, Gerald Woolacott, Tony Phillips, Percy Dennis.

© Gordon Bray

During 1991 eight keen golfers from the village decided to spend a few days away pursuing their sport. They set sail from Plymouth in November to play three days golf at Brest-Iroise in Brittany.

The success of this tour led them to form The Chittlehampton Golf Society. The inaugural meeting was held in November 1992 and the following were elected: Mike Dent (Chairman), David Billington (Secretary), Mark Jones (Treasurer), Robby Quick (Captain). Dave Reed has presented a trophy to the society which is now the prize for the largest annual competition.

Membership has grown steadily with the current membership standing at twenty two. The society plays a full year's programme with visits throughout the South West. Up to eighteen members and guests play on a day out. Many of the guests subsequently join, justifying the claim to be a friendly society where an enjoyable round of golf is more important than the result.

The society has continued to expand its own competitions for members, and now plays for the 'Billington Bowl' – a 36-hole competition, and a Knock-out Cup matchplay competition played locally at High Bullen Hotel throughout the summer.

TO WHOM IT MAY CONCERN

Please take this as confirmation that

MR JOHN ANDOW

Holed-in-One

at the 6th Hole of the Old Course at St Mellion

on Tuesday 24 March 1998

Fiona Walker
Golf Operations Manager
25.03.98

Above: *Golf Society at Carlyn Bay, 1997.*

Left to Right: Roger Gay, Kevin Sumers, Phil Evans, Mark Jones, Steve Darch, Brian Vanstone, Robby Quick, Dicko White, David (Bunker Billy) Billington.

© Cobbaton Photographic

SPORT

© Cobbaton Photographic

© Gordon Bray

Above: *Shove ha'penny Team, 1999.*

Left to right: Bill Westcott, Ern Ashton, June Matthews, Bob Slape, Peter Ash.

Right: *Maurice Matthews, 1989, South Molton Skittles League Champion and shove-ha'penny wizard.*

Above: *The 1998 golf winners.*
Left to right, back row: Roger Gay, Robin Smith, Dicko White, Dave Reed, Tony Holt, Brian Hazeldean, David Billington;
front row: Les Curtis, Mark Jones, Robby Quick.

Soccer has always been popular in the village although the first reports of football in the *Parish Magazine* during the 1890s actually refer to rugby. The following comes from *Chittlehampton Parish Magazine* January 1895:

The Football Club has made a very creditable start. Mr Veysey has most kindly given them the use of a sound piece of ground, and the Members have been practising steadily, sometimes even by moonlight. On Saturday, December 28th, they played their first game against an outside team from South Molton. They were beaten by one goal and two tries to nil, but there was no disgrace in such a defeat, for they played well, and shewed great promise of future success.

The magazine also notes in 1898 that: 'Our club have [sic] started a new jersey, not beautiful to look at but easy to distinguish.' The magazines record games against Beaford, Morchard Bishop, The Merry Boys, The Early Closers of Barnstaple, The Scarlet Runners, The Nondescripts and the Ilfracombe Good Templars. They also mention how 'Our Club' fared on all these occasions.

Below: *An account of the Rugby Club outing to Bideford from the* Parish Magazine, *January 1898.*

FOOTBALL.

On Saturday, November 13th, we journeyed to Westward Ho! and played a most stubbornly contested game with the United Services College. Never have our team appeared to such advantage. For the "first half" we led by a try and it was quite an open question as to whether we should remain victors till the last quarter of an hour, when the superior training and combination of the home side told its tale. We were eventually defeated by 1 goal and a try to a try, a very creditable result when we consider we were playing against a team which has every facility for practising every day together.

After the match we were most royally entertained at dinner, and were invited to stay for songs, etc., but had to make haste, as we had ordered our break at a given time, to get away to Bideford. All agreed when they reached Umberleigh safely by the last train, that they could not have had a more enjoyable outing.

On Saturday, November 20th, we played the 'Merry Boys,' at Barnstaple, a drawn game, each side obtaining a try. Space admits of no fuller description this month.

Above: *Chittlehampton Football Team 1934–35, winners of the Braunton Challenge Cup and League Cup.*
Left to right, back row: Fred Matthews, Philip Friendship, George Nott, Jack Featherstone, Jack Moor, Wilfred Baker, Wilfred Matthews, Percy Smoldon, Frank Squires;
seated: Reg Thomas, Bill Stone, Percy Baker, Frank Churchill; front: Gordon Burgess and 'Turkey' Lock.

Football, as we know it today, has certainly been played in the parish since the 1920s. Gordon Burgess recalls as a small boy playing football matches on Townsend field, next to Coles Bakery before the Second World War. Chittlehampton Association Football Club was reformed after the war in 1946–7, and the first match was played against the Army at Croyde. A *North Devon Journal* read:

At the Annual General Meeting of 1949, Chairman J.R. Burgess congratulated the club on its success in the past season. They had reached the final of the Braunton Challenge Cup, the semi final of the South Molton Cup and ended in fifth position in the North Devon League (third division). He also gave a balance sheet which showed a profit of £8.11s.8d. on the 1948–9 season.

North Devon Journal

Above: *Chittlehampton Football Team, 1947–48*
Left to right, back row: Johnny Grant, Budge Pickard, Jack Heddon, Everard Howard, Jack Toze, Fred Ford;
front row: Johnny Brace, Bill Stone, Roy Parker, Grenville Buckingham, Ron Darch.

Above: *1953–54 team and supporters.*
Left to right, back row: Fred Matthews, Jack Burgess, Mr Stenner, Wilf Matthews, Dick Whythe, Fred Darch;
centre: Dawn Phillips, Beattie Smoldon, Elsie Stone, Jill Smoldon, Margaret Darch, Percy Smoldon, John Darch, Lillian Whythe, B Matthews, Ern Short, Mrs Stenner, N Darch;
team back row: Ron Peters, Ron Darch, P C Ron Cox, Goalie Bill Pickard, Bill Stone, Johnny Grant, Ken Peters;
team front row: Shaver Ley, Mick Worth, Everard Howard, Clive Stenner, Grenville Buckingham;
front row: Eric Mayne, Stanley Mayne, Maurice Matthews, Pat Burgess, Ruth Stone, Hazel Vickery, Paul Grant, Alan Smoldon, Mick Webber, Terry Lethaby.

© Knights Photographic

Above: *The 1964 Football Club Dinner.*

Devon County Football Association

P R O G R A M M E

for

DEVON JUNIOR (SATURDAY)

C U P   F I N A L

Played at Okehampton on

Saturday 12th. May 1962

Kick off at 3.0 p.m.

C H I T T L E H A M P T O N

versus

P L Y M P T O N   A T H L E T I C

Referee: Mr. F. G. Fellowes, Plymouth
Linesmen: Mr. A. Hatten, Okehampton.
Mr. J. R. Rees, Holsworthy.

------- ----------

T H E   T E A M S
C H I T T L E H A M P T O N
(White Shirts / Black Shorts)

P. Dennis

R. Darch   G. Parkhouse

G. Chapman   J. Grant   R. Pincombe
                (Captain)
      M. Mathews   A. Smolden

T. Lethaby   K. Peters   G. Buckingham

            Reserves: R. Elstone
                      B. Murch
                      R. Peters

              T. Woodman   J. Crocker

L. Heard   D. Lowden

    R. Neetsonne   G. Quest

C. Burgess   T. Lee   H. Bazley

    G. Rule

              P. Daniels
            Reserves: R. Elford
                      G. Robertson

P L Y M P T O N   A T H L E T I C

(Amber and Black)

Progress of the Teams to the Final:-
Chittlehampton

October 7th. 1961 - Torrington   (A)Won 6-2
                    Reserves   (A) " 3-2
"   28th. 1961 - Brayford   (H) " 5-3
November 25th 1961 - Woolacombe (A) " 7-3
January 6th. 1962 - Combe Martin (H) " 4-3
February 10th.1962 - Hartland
April 14th   1962 - Bampton
                    (At Lynton) " 3-2

Plympton Athletic

.October 28th. 1961 - Woodland
                      Fort   (A) " 9-1
"   28th. 1961 - Tamar United(A) " 2-1
November 18th.1961 - Plymouth   (H) " 8-1
January 6th. 1962 - Plymouth
                    City   (H) " 4-0
February 10th 1962 - Dockland   (H) " 5-2
March 10th   1962 - Beacon Spurs(H) " 3-2
April 7th.   1962 - Yealm United(H)
April 21st   1962 - Tuckenhay (neutral)" 6-3

Home Club Notes

We extend a warm welcome to both the
competing Clubs and the visiting and
local Officials and Dignitaries. It is
our hope that we shall enjoy a good,
clean, sporting match and sincerely trust
this will not be the last time we shall
have the honour, and indeed pleasure, of
featuring such a fixture.
We are confident that few grounds offer
such very pleasant surrounding scenery
and a good playing pitch, and we hope our
visitors will remember their visit to
Okehampton with pleasure and a desire to
renew their acquaintance in the future.
We are also extremely pleased that His
Worship the Mayor, Councillor W. J.
                                   over/

It was round about this time that Bill Stone, who owned Upper Biddacott Farm then, offered Abbots Hill to be used as a football pitch. The club accepted gratefully, and were able to stay on the pitch until 1979 when the new playing field was built in the centre of the village.

Now established with a home ground and an entertainments committee, the club went on to hold its first Club Dinner in 1950.

In 1953, the club entered its most successful year. The team won the Braunton Cup, the Third Division and the Runners-Up League Cup. And within a few years – in 1960 – Everard Howard scored the first ever league goal with a header. The ball was made of leather, the laces flapped (painfully) and it was probably heavy with moisture from the pitch!

Two years later, Chittlehampton reached the Devon Junior Cup Final, and the following year scored 134 goals for the home side with only sixty six goals against.

Four names stand out as club players: John Grant, Ron Darch, Phil Quick and Alan Smoldon, each played over 500 games for Chittlehampton – now, that's club loyalty!

Above: *The 1963–64 Football Team.*

Left to right: Barry Murch, Chris Webber, Michael Ford, Stuart Beer, Peter Isaac, Ron Darch, Phil Quick (on shoulders), Terry Lethaby, Maurice Matthews, Brian Ward, Alan Smoldon.

THE BOOK OF CHITTLEHAMPTON

The new playing field was built in 1979 next to the village hall; it was such an undertaking that it was celebrated in a poem of sixty three verses by Edna Ford. Her *magnum opus* is written in dialect, and we wish there was room for more. The fund-raising events were many and varied and demonstrate much spirit and enthusiasm.

Mind you volks talked about having a
Playing Field yer More'n Forty Years ago.
I knaw for a fact that, that is true Cos
Doris Parkhouse told me so.

So a Committee was elected
To git this thing off the ground,
Mind you, they was frightened to death
when somebody said
But this could cost £6,000 pound.

One [event] was that there first Sponsored Walk
For weeks in the Village, twas all the talk,
Lots of Little Chilern, Mums and Dads too
Even Grannys I believe, said they'd zee
what they could do.

The money raised by that Walk
Was 432 pound
Seemed like might be possible, one day
To have their Playing Ground.

I know twad'n jis a Playing Field effort
We were only part of a team,
The whole community was involved
Wull, that's how it did seem.

There's far too much criticism and evil
In this world of ours today.
Lets just remind ourselves of what can
*   happen*
When volks work together in a friendly way.

So many volks have done so much
Their efforts can't be measured.
The Playing Field is now complete
And Always should be Treasured.

Edna Ford

Below: *Chittlehampton Playing Field, 1998.*

© Cobbaton Photographic

© Cobbaton Photographic

Above: *The 1998 Chittlehampton Under Eights.*
Left to right, back row: Matthew Jones, Charles Saunders, Alex Gilanders, Camron Ranson, Simon Lockyer;
front row: Ciaron Ranson, Liam Craze, Daniel Ardy, Charles Gilanders, Martyn Colley.

Below: *Chittlehampton Football Team 1993/4.*
Left to right, back row: M Matthews, B Norden, S Staker, P Willoughby, T Jones, C White, B Milton, I Pool;
front row: M Jones, T Davis, J Matthews, W Jones, J Thrower, M Latham.

Sheep-shearing competitors at The Old Vicarage.

CHITTLEHAMPTON PARISH MAGAZINE.

CRICKET CLUB BALANCE SHEET.

SUBSCRIPTIONS

	£	s.	d.
Venble. Archdeacon Seymour	1	0	0
Honble. M. Rolle......	1	0	0
Honble A. Fortescue	1	0	0
Canon Trefusis		10	6
Miss C. Hodgetts ...		10	0
Mr. G. Dawe		10	0
Mr. T. Cardus		5	0
Rev. A. Spicer		5	0
Capt. Edwards		5	0
Mr. Skynner		4	0
- J. M. Mortimer		5	0
- A. E. Skynner ...		5	0
- H. C. Watts		5	0
- F. Veysey		5	0
- S. Vickery		5	0
- J. M. Hartnoll...		2	6
- S. Howard		2	6
- F. Smallridge ...		2	6
- J. Thompson ...		2	6
- W. Denley		2	6
- D. Rawle		2	6
Members	2	4	0
Balance from last year		5	0
Collection after Annual Supper	1	0	2½
	£10	18	8½

EXPENSES.

	£	s.	d.
3 Balls at 5/-		15	0
Rent of Field	2	0	0
Materials for Pavilion, per J. R. Howard	5	17	3
Ironwork, per Mr. Hunt		14	2½
Labour........................		11	6
Postage and Printing		4	6
Sundries		4	2
Dinner Expenses................		5	6
Balance in hand		6	7
	£10	18	8½

THE CRICKET CLUB.

On May 18th, we journeyed to West Buckland and played the School (with Masters). It was a most enjoyable match, though the wind was cold and the ball seemed to have more than its usual amount of "sting". The School batted first on a hard and rather fiery wicket, and ran up a score of 134, Messrs. Paul and Davies, and a young and promising batsman, G. Orchard, being the chief contributors. The innings closed at 5.30: thus, after deducting the interval, leaving Chittlehampton three-quarters of an hour for play. In that time they managed to score 92 for 3 wickets, the match ending at 6.30, in a highly creditable draw in our favour. We may say, all did their best for the result, though the fielding was not quite so smart as it might be. Never have we seen Mr. Knott in such a merry mood with the willow.

Our ground has suffered rather in consequence of the dry weather, and needs assiduous rolling. We hope that all members will come forward and volunteer to assist us in the evenings, and that it will not be allowed to fall wholly on two or three willing hands.

A Meeting of the Members of the Cricket Club was held in the School, on April 16th, at which the Archdeacon was again elected President, Mr. Gegg, Captain, Mr. J. Mortimer, Vice-Captain. The Members have been diligently watering and rolling the newly laid ground, and the pitch ought to be in good order on Whitsun Tuesday, when the annual struggle between Married and Single will take place.

LADIES v. GENTLEMEN OF CHITTLEHAMPTON.

Played at Chittlehampton, on Sept. 4th. The Gentlemen batting, bowling, & fielding left-handed.

Ladies.

1st Innings.		2nd Innings.	
Miss A. Seymour, b J Vickery	7	b J Vickery	23
- Carrie Watts, b B Hulland	9	st, b R Seymour	0
- H Seymour, c M Seymour b J Vickery			
- G Burgess, b J Vickery	4	b B Hulland	0
- M Burgess, b B Hulland	0	did not bat	7
- Cherry Watts, c M Seymour b J Vickery		c M Seymour b R Seymour	3
- E Seymour, run out	1	b B Hulland	3
- A Veysey, c J Vickery b B Hulland	1	not out	1
- F Vickery, c E Howard b J Vickery	3	c J Vickery b B Hulland	13
- E Marshall, not out	0	b R Seymour	1
- M Goss, b J Vickery	1	run out	0
	1	c M Seymour b B Hulland	0
	34		44

Gentlemen.

1st Innings.		2nd Innings.	
M R Seymour, b Carrie Watts	23	c & b M Burgess	22
E Howard, b Carrie Watts	1	b Carrie Watts	1
J Vickery, c M Burgess b Carrie Watts	4	b Carrie Watts	0
B Hulland, b Carrie Watts	2	b M Burgess	0
R Seymour, c Cherry Watts b Carrie Watts	0	b M Burgess	0
R Stephens, b Carrie Watts	0	lbw b H Seymour	2
E A Seymour, b Carrie Watts	7	b Mary Burgess	4
L V Edwards, not out	0	b Carrie Watts	6
C Vickery, b Carrie Watts	0	not out	0
A G Seymour, c M Goss b M Burgess	1	b Carrie Watts	14
W Burgess, b M Burgess	0	b Carrie Watts	1
Extras	1	Extras	1
	39		51

Exracts from the Parish Magazine, *1895–1905.*

The oldest recorded game in the parish is cricket, which was established in 1875. Early *Parish Magazines* show the scorecards, functions and the annual club expenses: Batting gloves cost 5s.6d., balls 5s. each, and rent for the field was £2.

The team played about nine fixtures a season increasing to sixteen in 1904. The clergy always seemed to open the batting, whether they scored runs or not, though the Reverend Gegg was a good cricketer, taking lots of wickets and recording eighty nine not out on 7 August 1897. Often both sides would bat twice in an afternoon, but we have to remember they probably only had sheep to help mow the field, including the pitch. Nets, however, were encouraged, as testified by the *Parish Magazine*:

Our net has come and has been in use the last three Practice-nights. It is hoped that many of our Members will now avail themselves of the more favourable conditions of becoming efficient in the game.

The field on which they played was next to the barn, behind the Old Vicarage which overlooks the village.

Cricketing history comes in short bursts, presumably because land for a cricket pitch was harder to come by. They played on the Vicarage pitch in the early years of the century and again after the First World War. Geoff Birchall remembers as a boy in the early 1950s, the smell of stinging nettles as he walked to tea in the old barn next to that pitch. The first recorded century appears in the *North Devon Journal*:

Chittlehampton Captain on form.

Scoring 92 in boundary hits (eight sixes and 11 fours) Gordon Burgess took a century off the home bowlers at Chulmleigh on Wednesday in 47 minutes. Chittlehampton were able to declare at 139 for 5 and won by 66 runs.

When Burgess went to the crease the score was 6 for 1. He and Darch put on 130 runs for the second wicket. This was the first century to be scored on Chulmleigh's new ground.

R. Darch	b. Caws	26
J. Squire	b. Southcombe ...	5
G. Burgess	retired	101
G. Stuckey	b.Caws	0
R. Mules	b. Short	0
R. Birchall	not out	1

C. Stenner, G. Sylvester, G. Buckingham, I. Pratt, and S. Warren did not bat.

Below: *The Old Vicarage garden where cricket was played in the early 1950s.*

© Cobbaton Photographic

Above: *Chittlehampton versus Ashford, 24 August 1948.*

Left to right, standing: Fred Glover, Douglas Bale, Everard Howard, Gordon Sylvester, Budge Pickard, J R Burgess;

seated: Gordon Stuckey, Ron Darch, Bill Stone, Gordon Burgess (Captain), Bert Phillips, Ron Birchell

Right: *John E Andrew out ratting with his father before the First World War.*

At a match against North Molton, J R Burgess was umpiring and the captain, Gordon Burgess, remonstrated with his grandfather over a 'caught behind' decision only to be told 'I didn't want to give him out, he's an awfully nice chap!'

The following comes from the *North Devon Journal* of 1950:

Chittlehampton Cricket Club have decided to change their name to Taw Valley Cricket Club.

This was agreed at the annual general meeting on Wednesday, when it was reported that the club has been unable to find a suitable ground, but have been offered a pitch at Umberleigh Barton by Mr. John E.

Above: *Taw Valley Cricket Club, 1951.*
Left to right, standing: Umpire J R Burgess, T Kennedy, David Somerville, Berty Phillips, Revd Andrews, Gordon Sylvester, Jack Nutt;
seated: Ron Birchell, Rocker Smoldon, Gordon Burgess, F Norton, M Caws.

Below: *A lady cricketer of the early 1900s.*

Chittlehampton Cricket Club was revived in 1978, for a few seasons in a field on Everard Howard's farm, behind the allotments. They travelled to Barnstaple's recreational ground, and even played a season on a bumpy village football pitch.

The main bowlers from existing records of 1978–81 were Michael Ford, Stephen Darch, Peter Jones and Chris Walters. No centuries were made but a few fifties were scored by Trevor and Barry Mayne, Ron and Steve Darch, Dave Reed (the driving force), Colin Bawden, Michael Peters and Gary Phillips.

Too many fixtures without a decent home pitch made life very difficult and it became impossible to continue to receive guests. The Club folded again having survived only five years until 1983, although occasional pub games were organised by Dave Reed.

Then in 1996 another attempt was made at a revival. Almost immediately afterwards Higher Biddacott Farm and all its surrounding land went up for auction. It was too good an opportunity to be missed, but where would the club raise funds in order to go to the auction?

The Foundation for Sports and the Arts donated £14,000 enabling the Cricket and Sports Club to buy a field.

About a hundred years ago, the ladies were challenged by the men, the gentlemen to bat, bowl and field left-handed.

This challenge was taken up again in 1997 by the girls who were willing to compete.

Regular coaching and practices were organised and the Chittlehampton Ladies Cricket Team was formed. The women were victorious, although a hundred runs were deducted from the men for swearing in front of a lady and it was probably the sixteenth batswoman who scored the winning run!

In 1999 the club played a Ladies versus Under-14 Colts side; a good village day, including a BBQ, and a fun game, but the ladies' tactics were slightly dubious. It transpired that the lady wicket-keeper had embarrassed the Colts' best batsman by asking if he was 'wearing a box' and did it 'fit properly'. He was out first ball, demonstrating that the ladies' win-at-any-cost strategy was successful.

© Cobbaton Photographic

Above: *The first Ladies' Cricket Team and coach, 1997.*
Left to right, back row: Andrea Walters, Debbie Mogford, Claire Campbell, Phillipa Shanahan, Jan Wyatt, Sandra Steel, Charlotte Davis, Sharon Howard, Carole Henderson-Begg, Debbie Isaac, Joy Cottey, Mary Parker;
seated: Lynn Jones, Tracy Craze (Captain), John Andow (Coach), Jo Jones, Jenny Peters.

The arrival of a heavy roller for any village cricket team trying to flatten a cow field into a cricket wicket is a momentous occasion. The roller was given to them by Eton School; all the Club had to do was collect it. A large truck was driven to Eton and the roller safely loaded by JCB for the long, slow journey home. The roller weighed over two tons; so how to get the monster off the high-bed truck? The worried driver was told 'no problem' by Preston and Tim Isaac of the Cobbaton Combat Museum. They lifted it sweetly off the truck on to firm ground with their tank recovery vehicle, ready for the two-mile drive back to Chittlehampton and into its new home on Abbots Hill.

Right: The tank recovery vehicle lifts the heavy roller off the lorry.

Below: Fran Campbell rides the roller from Cobbaton Combat Museum into town.

Above: *Chittlehampton v Chairman's Invitation XI on Abbots Hill, 1997.*

Left to right, back row: Mark Popplewell, Clive Rowe, Tracy Craze, Jim Butcher, Nigel Grimshire, Steve Madge, Chris White, Trevor Frost, Mark Reeves, Roger Gay, Ron Jewell, Gerald Luscombe;

front row: Ben Newton, Robby Quick, Robin Smith, Robby Murch, Charles Coleville (Sky TV), John Andow (Chairman), Steve Darch, Mark Jones, David Billington, Richard Walters.

Sky Sports programme 'The Pavilion End' decided to make a feature of 'Cow Field to Cricket Pitch', and visited the ground in its early stages to film progress. Programme host Charles Coleville played in a Selection XI against the village and his century was duly recorded.

Only three players have scored a century for Chittlehampton since the 1950s. Robin Smith scored 126 not out at Combe Martin in 1996, John Andow's best was 146 against Molland in the first match on Abbots Hill the following year and in the summer of 2000, in his first game for the club, Mark Young scored 102 not out at home against Bishops Nympton.

The club has over fifty participating playing members and has a full fixture list of nearly forty games a year which includes eighteen home games on Abbots Hill.

The new petanque terrain – already popular – overlooks Abbots Hill which is a beacon point used for village bonfire nights and royal celebrations.

Left: *The site for the petanque (boules) terrain overlooking the Beacon Point and the cricket field on Abbots Hill.*

SPORT

Facing page: *Bonfire Night, 1998, on the Beacon Point at Abbots Hill.*

Right: *The Twinning Association play petanque with their boules, a gift from Baron-Sur-Odon, France*

Below: *The new petanque site comes slowly into being.*

Bottom: *Cricket match on Abbots Hill, 1998.*

© Cobbaton Photographic

Chittlehampton from Homedown Cross.

Conclusion

There is nothing revolutionary here – no claims to outstanding fame – no grim secrets revealed. The book stands as a clear demonstration of community with its own identity and its own characteristics. Fierce allegiances are maintained and opinions divided and sub-divided, but these are acknowledged and respected so that the parish can still stand together in the melting pots of church, pub and playing field. Events throughout the year bring together locals and 'incomers', political rivals, arts and agriculture, those across the financial divide and even the young and old!

So perhaps there is a conclusion – that the parish of long ago that cared and was responsible for its own is still doing so, though perhaps in a less material way.

That's good. That's as it should be.

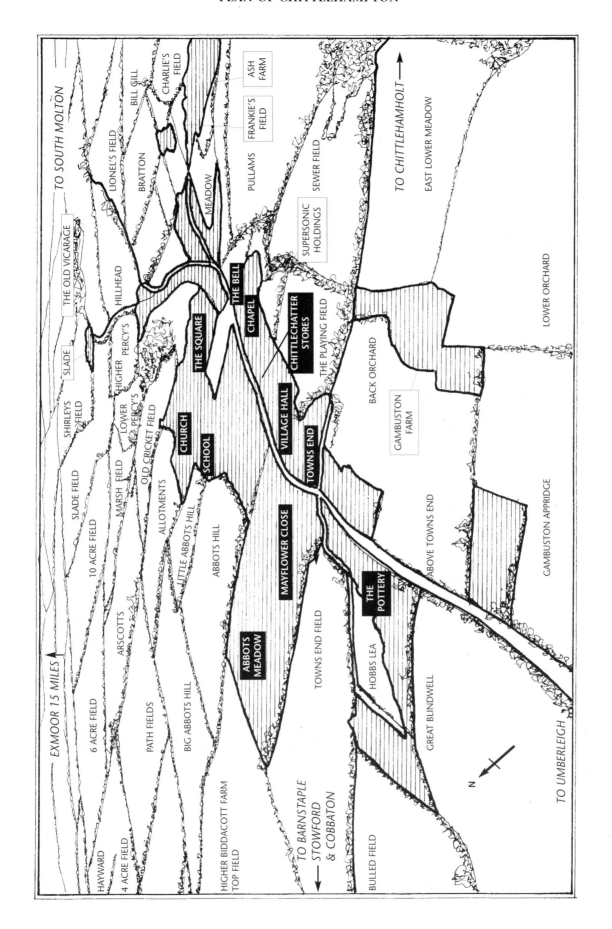

Donations

Devon Rural Action for the Environment

North Devon District Council

European Regional Development Fund through Devon County Council

Chittlehampton Parish Council

Chittlehampton Twinning Association

Parish Fund-raising Events

The Lord Clinton

The Countess of Arran

Colonel and Mrs M W Maxse

J H Thomas

Murch Bros.

Picture Credits

A M I Aerial Photos   01582 793007

Beaford Archive   01271 388607

Tony Freeman   01271 324000

Bath Photographic   01237 479331

Knight Photographic   01271 371776

North Devon Journal   01271 343064

John Andow and Stella Levy at Cobbaton Photographic 01769 540602

Thanks also to Bray Leino Advertising for their help in scanning many of the images in this book.

Subscribers

Richard Ackland, Farnham, Surrey
Angela M. Adams, Landkey, Devon
Mrs Meta Alford, Linlithgow, Scotland
Paul and Pauline Alford, The Green,
    Umberleigh, Devon
Matthew and Lucy Alford, The Green,
    Umberleigh, Devon
Lyall and Hazel Alford, Chittlehampton,
    Devon
Peter and Julia Ash, Chittlehampton, Devon
Beverly Ashford, Chittlehampton, Devon
Guy and Rachel Barnard (née Murch), formerly
    of Umberleigh, Devon
Martin Barr, Dee Why, NSW, Australia
Mrs Joyce E. Barrans (née White), Barnstaple,
    Devon
Mr and Mrs Barrett, Warkleigh, Devon
Mrs Barrow, Homestead, Umberleigh, Devon
Joan N. Barrow (née Lethbridge), South
    Molton, Devon
Mr Brian Beard, Chittlehampton, Devon
Mr Stewart Beer, St Giles
Roger C. Bickley, Umberleigh, Devon
Lyn, Gayle and David Billington,
    Chittlehampton, Devon
Pat Bissett (née Burgess), Barnstaple, Devon
Mrs Patricia C. Borley
Freda Bourne, Umberleigh, Devon
Bruce and Audrey Bowden, Chittlehampton,
    Devon
Mr and Mrs J. M. Braid, West Stowford,
    Chittlehampton, Devon
Noel Branch, Umberleigh, Devon
Joan Brayley, Atherington, Devon
Angela and Michael Bridges, Chittlehampton,
    Devon
Colin Browne, Cobbaton, Chittlehampton,
    Devon
Roger Brownson, Bridgnorth, Shropshire
Richard Brownson, Bideford, Devon
Joy Bruce, Chittlehampton, Devon
John Bryant Skinner Jr., San Jose, California
B. and M. Burgess, Atherington, Devon
Gordon and Kathleen Burgess,
    Chittlehampton butcher for over 40 years
Arthur Burgess Skinner Jr., San Francisco
J. Burned, Christchurch, Dorset
K. J. Burrow, Bucks Cross, Devon

Sybil Cardy (née Hooper), Exmouth, Devon
Loraine and Bill Castle, Chittlehampton,
    Devon
B. Chambers, Chittlehampton, Devon
Chittlehampton Twinning Association
Barry and Sharon Clemens, Chittlehampton,
    Devon
John Clutterbuck M.B.E., Umberleigh, Devon
Roger and Ros Cockram, Chittlehampton,
    Devon
Albert E. Cook, Filleigh, Devon
Stephen W. Cooke, Umberleigh, Devon
Jan Cornish (née Courtenay), Crowborough,
    Sussex
Angus and Joy Cottey, Chittlehampton, Devon
Mark, Tracey, Bianca and Liam Craze,
    Chittlehampton, Devon
Marian J. Cross, Edwalton, Nottingham
Mrs N. Darch, Chittlehampton, Devon
Ron and Marg Darch, South Molton, Devon
Nigel, Alison, Tim and Charlotte Davies,
    East Stowford, Umberleigh, Devon
Eileen Dolling (née Burton), Chulmleigh,
    Devon
Robert and Judith Domleo, Fisherton Farm,
    Atherington, Devon
Peter Down, Chittlehampton, Devon
Victor and Edith Drummond, Frimley Green,
    Surrey
Diane and Alan Drummond, Hillcrest,
    Umberleigh, Devon
Margaret R. Eden, Southampton, Hampshire
Marilyn A. Eden, Buckhurst Hill, Essex
Nick and Kate Edwards, Peaslake, Surrey
Simon and Lizzie Edwards, Oxford
Bill and Marian Edwards, Cobbaton,
    Umberleigh, Devon
Barbara and George Elmore, Newlands Farm
Frederick A. Elworthy, Swimbridge, Devon
Mr and Mrs G. G. Ettery, At Rackmead Terrace
    for 45 years
Marilyn Facey, Filleigh, Devon
Martin and Sara Fisher, Elston, Newark
Miriam Fitter, Dolton, Devon
Stephen Ford, Umberleigh, Devon (formerly of
    Chittlehampton)
John and Edna Ford, Umberleigh, Devon
    (formerly of Chittlehampton)

Raymond Ford, Seaton, Devon (born in
  Chittlehampton 1961)
Jess Fubini, Chittlehampton, Devon
Edna M. Glover, Barnstaple, Devon
Mrs Elizabeth Mary Gover (née Thorne),
  Barnstaple, Devon
Janice V. Gratton, Chandlersford, Hampshire
John and Cynthia Greaves, Stowford, Devon
Mr and Mrs John Guard, Exeter, Devon
George Harris, formerly of Whey Farm,
  Umberleigh, Devon
Victor J. Harris, Chittlehampton, Devon
Mr Len and Mrs Margaret Hazelden (née
  Ettery), Banstead, Surrey
Ann Denise Headon, Chittlehampton, Devon
Shirley J. Heal, Slade, Chittlehampton, Devon
Suzanne Henbest, Tunbridge Wells, Kent
Kyle Henderson-Begg, Chittlehampton, Devon
Gregor Henderson-Begg, Chittlehampton,
  Devon
Ruari and Nicola Henderson-Begg,
  Chittlehampton, Devon
Dugan Henderson-Begg, Chittlehampton, Devon
Carole Henderson-Begg, Chittlehampton, Devon
The Hickman family, Whey Farm, Umberleigh,
  Devon
Mr John Hirst, Llandovery, Carmarthenshire
Mary A. F. Holcombe
Mike and Glenda Hopkins, Stowford,
  Chittlehampton, Devon
W. J. Hosking, Chittlehampton, Devon
Philip Howard, Chittlehampton, Devon
Marian Howard, Chittlehampton, Devon
Nichola Hussell (née Smoldon),
  Chittlehampton, Devon
Ivan, Edna and Paul Huxtable, Umberleigh,
  Devon
Brian, Rauchele and William Huxtable,
  Umberleigh, Devon
Bryan R. Huxtable, Barnstaple, Devon
D. P. and G. M. Hyde, Brimley,
  Chittlehampton, Devon
Preston Isaac, Cobbaton, Chittlehampton,
  Devon
Martin and Cathryn Ives, Chittlehampton,
  Devon
David and Helena Johnson, Great Deptford
  Farm, Umberleigh, Devon
Kyran David Jones, Chittlehampton, Devon
Matthew Joshua Jones, Chittlehampton,
  Devon
Mark and Lynn Jones, Chittlehampton, Devon
Mr and Mrs Kean, Bracknell, Berkshire

Pauline R. Kerslake, Bishops Nympton, Devon
Mrs Muriel King, London
Hilda A. Kingdon, Barnstaple, Devon
Robin and Joan Lawrence, Chittlehampton,
  Devon
Mrs J. Leach, The Stores, Umberleigh, Devon
Edwin John Lee, Chapel Cottage,
  Chittlehampton, Devon
Joyce Kathleen Lee, Chapel Cottage,
  Chittlehampton, Devon
Richard Lethbridge, Chittlehamholt, Devon
May Lethbridge, Chittlehampton, Devon
Saul and Caroline Levy, London
Justin, Jamie and Maxwell Levy, USA
Dorcas Elizabeth Lines,
Sue M. Luscombe, Chittlehampton, Devon
Mrs D. M. Mackenzie, Hudscot 1977–1991
Charles and Heather Manktelow, The Rising
  Sun, Umberleigh, Devon
Cherise Mansi, Perth, Australia
John and Jill Mansi, Chittlehampton, Devon
Jenny Martin, Weston-Super-Mare, Somerset
Derek and Margaret Matthews,
  Chittlehampton, Devon
Linda Moore, Bickington, Devon
David Morgan, Brussels, Belgium
Mr and Mrs C. W. Morgan, Chittlehamholt,
  Devon
Michael Murch, Mill Hill, London
Robert Murch, Dorridge, Umberleigh, Devon
Patrick H. Murch, Dorridge, Umberleigh, Devon
Catherine Murch, Dorridge, Umberleigh, Devon
Edna and Dan Murch, Chittlehampton, Devon
Mr David Murch, Little Torrington, Devon
Anto and Di Murch, Chittlehampton, Devon
R. Newton, Chittlehampton, Devon
The North Devon Athenaeum
Rob and Ann Page, Winson Farm,
  Chittlehampton, Devon
John and Brigitte Palmer, Chittlehampton, Devon
Emily and Alicia Parker, Chittlehampton, Devon
C. J. and M. Parker, Chittlehampton, Devon
Sallie Parker, Chittlehampton, Devon
Godfrey and Greta Parkhouse,
  Chittlehampton, Devon
Nigel Passmore, Vancouver, Canada
Vella Passmore, Ilfracombe, Devon
Frank and Maxine Pawley, Stowford,
  Chittlehampton, Devon
P. Pawley and A. Pawley-Kean,
  Chittlehampton, Devon
Rob and Valerie Paynter, Chittlehampton,
  Devon

Jean Penny, Huntworth, Somerset.
Step-daughter of Victor Lethbridge
Oran Perrett, Chittlehampton, Devon
Ross Perrett, Chittlehampton, Devon
Mrs S. Peters, Chittlehampton, Devon
Rosemary Peters, Chittlehampton, Devon
Nannette A. and Kenneth B. Peters,
Chittlehampton, Devon
Colin J. Peters, London
Neal Phillips, Luxborough
Gary Phillips, Brackley
Bob and Ruth Phillips, Chittlehampton, Devon
Pamela Philp, Umberleigh, Devon
Mrs Irene Pickard, Chittlehampton, Devon
Mr Alwyn and Marion Pickard, Mariansleigh,
Devon
Gordon and Jo Pickering, Windsor
Pat and Margaret Pidler, North Furze,
Chittlehampton, Devon
Margaret Pincombe, Chittlehampton, Devon
Cathrine Poulton, Umberleigh, Devon
Dr Chev. K. G. Powell Mackenzie K.L.J., D.C.P.,
O.St.G., Hudscot 1977–
Malcolm W. Pratt, Queanbeyan, N.S.W.,
Australia
Mr and Mrs David Reed, Chittlehampton,
Devon
Wendie S. Reed Do Couto, Chittlehampton,
Devon/Portugal
Harry and Pat Richardson and Rose Eyre,
Chittlehampton, Devon
Barbara J. Roy, Sudbury, Canada
Mrs. Sanders, Park Gate, Umberleigh, Devon
Jon and Marilyn Saunders, Chittlehampton,
Devon
Chris and Jean Saunders, Andover, Hampshire
Mr Peter Seage, South Molton, Devon
Mr Nelson Seldon, Cobbaton, Devon
Mr and Mrs Shallcross, Umberleigh, Devon
Mr Mick Shearlaw, Toits, Umberleigh, Devon
Pauline Ann Sheath (née Lethaby),
Chittlehampton, Devon
Mr Peter D. and Mrs Sally P. Shepherd (née
Ettery), Chittlehampton, De
Sally and Ron Sidaway,
Mr N. P. Sidnell, (Evacuee) White Gates,
Chittlehampton, Devon
Margaret Sidnell, Evacuee from Hackney,
London
Bridget Simmons, Chittlehampton, Devon
Sheila Sinclair, The Croft, Chittlehampton, Devon
Robert J. Skinner, San Francisco
Cynthia Skinner, San Francisco

Catherine Skinner Auby, Sunnyvale, California
Lorna Slocombe (née Huxtable), Barnstaple,
Devon
Hazel Mary Small (née Eastman),
Chittlehampton, Devon
Alan and Jen Smoldon, Chittlehampton, Devon
Stephen Snell, Chittlehampton, Devon
Jayne Snell, Chittlehampton, Devon
Lorna Southcombe, Chittlehampton, Devon
D. Joan Squire, Barnstaple, Devon
Sharon A. Standen, Gunn, Devon
Alexandra M. Steele, Chittlehampton, Devon
Mr and Mrs Peter Stevens, Middlesborough,
Teeside
Sidey G. Stevens, Torrington, Devon
George Stuckey, Homelea, Eastacombe, Devon
John H. and Heather B. Thomas, Umberleigh,
Devon
Jill Tillett (née Smoldon), Exeter, Devon
Tony, St Teara, Chittlehampton, Devon
Julie T. Tuckett, Crediton, Devon
Annie Tudball
Mrs Eliza Beth Twining, Chittlehampton, Devon
Sandra Uher, Umberleigh, Devon
Mrs K. Wadham, Crediton, Devon
Gerald W. C. Waldon, Little Deptford,
Umberleigh, Devon
Ian and Rachel Waldron, Chittlehampton,
Devon
Rob and Sharyn Walker, Umberleigh, Devon
Judith C. Walker (née Mayne),
Chittlehampton, Devon
John F. W. Walling, Newton Abbot, Devon
Victoria, Gerry, Jazmin and Joseph Walsh,
Cairns, Australia
Chris Walters, Alderney, Channel Islands
Christopher Walters, Torrington, Devon
David and Rosemary Warren, Chittlehampton,
Devon
John and Maureen Watt, South Molton, Devon
Roger and Jenny Watts, Filleigh, Devon
Patrick John Webber
Susan E. Webber, Chittlehampton, Devon
Jim Wheaton, formerly of Stowford,
Near Chittlehampton, Devon
Chalky White, South Molton, Devon
Dick White, South Molton, Devon
Revd and Mrs J. White, Uplyme, Devon
Mr Alan J. White (Chalkie), Chittlehampton,
Devon
Peter G. Whittaker, Wimbledon
Mary P. Wilson, Umberleigh, Devon
Mrs Shirley Wood, Chittlehampton, Devon